Blood
and
Roses

A Devotional for
Aphrodite and Venus

Edited by Rebecca Buchanan

BIBLIOTHECA ALEXANDRINA

Cover image: "An Offering to Venus" by John William Godward, 1912. Public domain, image courtesy of wikimedia commons.

Aphrodite by K.S. Roy

Dedication

To the Foam-Born
Unfettered Rose
Lover Warrior Mother Creatrix

Table of Contents

Poetry

Essays

Myths

Rites and Recipes

Introduction

by Rebecca Buchanan

Aphrodite and Venus are complex Goddesses. The same may be said, of course, of any Deity. When it comes to Deities associated with love or sex, though, too many fall back on caricature when trying to explain or understand such Powers: they are all lusty bubbleheads or consumed with materialist desires, or, worse, frivolous and cruel, given to playing with human hearts for their own amusement.

That is not Aphrodite, nor is it Venus. (Nor is that Hathor or Bast or Freyja or Ishtar or Aenghus or Xochiquetzal or Kama or Dzydzilelya.*) Rather, they are Goddesses of immense power and deep passions, who can be kind and angry, wise and stubborn, cosmic in their transcendence and intimate in their immanence.

Given their complexity, it is no surprise that their devotees each experience them a bit differently. There is overlap, certainly; there is a reason that so many refer to Aphrodite as the Golden One or the Golden Goddess, and that so many speak of her warmth and compassion. For others, though, She is a Mistress who demands total devotion, or the Mother of the Sea who holds us safe in her eternal waters, or a Power responsible for maintaining the cohesion of creation itself. Similarly, many refer to Venus as the Mother of

Rome, and so experience Her as deeply maternal; for others, She is the Mistress of the Garden (especially flower gardens). For still others, these Goddesses are a force of righteous anger to be justifiably feared, or a loving friend to shield a broken heart, or a Power so immense that they can only be even partially understood through the symbolism of myths and dreams.

Given the complexity of these Goddesses, and the varied ways in which She manifests in the lives of Her devotees, the poems and essays and myths and rites here included reflect that very complexity. Many of their devotees see them as distinct entities, a Power unto themselves; others see Aphrodite and Venus as one and the same, as unique cultural manifestations of the same divinity; still others see Her as an aspect or name for the universal Power which inspires and manifests love in all its forms.

Whatever your relationship with the Goddess/es, it is our hope that you will find the words here both inspirational and inspired, and wholly reverent.

Rebecca Buchanan
Summer 2017

*Respectively, Egyptian, Egyptian, Norse, Mesopotamian/Sumerian, Celtic, Aztec, Hindu, and Polish Deities.

Poetry

Venus Frigida by Peter Paul Rubens

Adonis: The Invocation

by Robert F. Gross

what a hideous answer
to have his cry   raving naked grasping his
prayer
answered by another his
still young and this death an impossibility
            (he thought still but each
moment
more terrified)

it was even as up and down in furious embrace

called upon her
          turned rank mad and wrung
his body
plastered with raging moments
          with gestures convulsive
    eyes taut

then confused cursed weeping   rage of rage
    unanswered

and then kisses
according to what   he thought   an action of
the other   a wound redoubled
    deepened   in open
abandoned imagination

fearful frenzied guiltless
                    the wounded hunter's
                              furiously
moving mouth
supplications   from within
a clearing
        memories
                of thrice-blessed immoderate
pleasure   breaking
pain   almost unbridled   bliss
in the wound   helped to salve
        for the moment
                        radiance
                into his mind
                his madness split
giving himself over as
                wave broke over
                morning star
        unaware
                she stood there
                stood armored and still

 a final   cry spilt from him
                bled
                from exhausted countenance
and famished caress
                    still

The Anatomical Venus

by Gareth Writer-Davies

if I could see
through your skin

would the rouse
soon pall

the mon
of the pubis

the brain
tight in bud, upon a narrow stem

automatics
satisfy the sense of breathing

but with an odour of medicine
we make co-habitation

with the mortal sphere of female form

the uterus
(motive)

umbra
(like blossom, upon the heart)

secrets
of bedfellows (who know too little or too much)

if I could see
through your skin

I would
with modesty, avert the candid eye

Venus
there are ugly things, we should know

Aphrodite

by Gareth Writer-Davies

if there was so much love in the world
would the carnal function

wither
like a frosted bud

the winter reminder
that each flower contains the seed of its own decay

Aphrodite
you have the lust to re-produce the Spring

the featherbed
wherein creatures burrow and toil

to break darkness
you have taken me deep Aphrodite

the idle jack
who mastered but one trade (the act of love)

the march hare
comes in from the field snorting

Spring is here
steal pleasance whilst you can

Aphrodite: From the Depths

by Gerri Leen

The sea spawns monsters
All shapes and sizes
Long and lean, clear like jelly
With razor-sharp teeth, or stings of death
But none of them
These sea monsters
Bring as much misery as I have

For all the joy love bestows
So much evil has been done in my name

Poseidon spit me out
Made me beautiful, gave me form
Set me loose on the land
Bordering his lovely, watery domain
I tripped, I faltered
Any who asked
Got their heart's desire

Some stayed together, others split apart easily
But the rest? Love can turn monstrous

Show me your great white sharks
Saltwater crocodiles
Barracuda and stonefish
When lovers grasp too tightly
Love strangles like a kraken's hold

Cuts more deeply than a ray's spine
And poisons like a blue-ringed octopus

Love wisely, hold loosely, give easily
Make of love a joy, not a killing thing

Show me I was not a fool to stay on land

Aphrodite, Lady of Change

by Merit Brokaw

When you are balanced,
And yet unable to move,
I call that stagnation.
So I rock your world,
Forcing a change,
For I am about growth.
Lover, friend, enemy,
Any one of them
Can be my messenger.
You will listen and learn
One way or another.
Like Artemis, I am independent.
I make my own decisions.
I am my own guide.
None can stay my hand
Unless I desire it.
Move. Or I will move you.

Aphrodite Rising

by Anne Graue

Somewhere in
the waters
off Cyprus
lies my virginity,
submerged beneath
waves — years of
might-have-beens
and what ifs —
waiting to lose itself
again and again
in the rapture of water
to captured plane pilots,
drowned ship captains,
or sailors who mistake
manatees for mermaids
and sex for true love,
drink and cast
themselves into
the sea foam still
churning with
pomegranates — home
to dolphin gangs,
seafarers, Magellans
and gods — cockle
shells, silver
bells, and pretty
maids — all in a row.

Aphrodite's Birthplace

by Anne Graue

I [Aphrodite] should find some favour with the sea,
for in its holy depths in days gone by from sea-foam
I was formed, and still from foam I take my name in
Greece. — Ovid, *The Metamorphoses*

The rocks are jagged and the wind whips up
the waves, finds us standing on smooth stones
in strong heat staring at the bluest air
above and the sea crawling in with hands
stretched out within summoning wind shifts
heaving closer and pulling back. Away from
Paphos, the foam churns as it always has
bringing with it the goddess's answer
to life, Eros and Himeros in tow,
and we stand there wondering what to do
with all of this free time in the wide world,
staring at the rock of Aphrodite
or so they say to bring the tourists here
for swimming, ice cream, and a foamy beer.

Aphrodite's Gifts

by Merit Brokaw

Your gift to man is love.
Not only Romantic love
But also between kin.
There is maternal and paternal love.
Love of nature.
Love born of friendship.
Love of one's fellow man.
Love of pets,
Love of one's homeland,
And love of self.

Your gift to man is beauty.
Beauty is in the eye of the beholder.
It is subjective and can be found
In the exotic and in the mundane.
It can be found with laughter
And with tears.
It can be internal or external.
Beauty can build one up or
Tear one down.

Your gift to man is strife.
Strife born of jealousy.
Strife born of desire.
From envy that turns one green
To despair all covered in black
To chaotic lustful impulses.

You upset the status quo
To force man to grow.

Your gift to man is sex.
Sex with a loved one.
Sex with a stranger.
Whether done alone or
or within a group.
Painful or kinky or vanilla.
With male or female partners.

Your gift to man is anger.
Anger born of righteousness.
Anger born of indignation.
From vision clearing
To seeing nothing but red
As it shows a depth of feeling.

Your gifts to man are many
They bring pleasure,
They bring pain.
They let us know we are alive.

Golden Lady, Heavenly One, Mother of All
I hail thee lovely Aphrodite
I thank thee for thy gifts.

Aphrodite Soteira

by Merit Brokaw

Told by a friend to a friend about a friend …
A long time ago, in a time far away,
a merchant made a fortunate find
in the last port before homeward bound:
Archaic in style and only a span high,
a statuette of Aphrodite,
patroness of Naukratis, his hometown.

Carefully wrapped in rugs,
tied securely to the main mast,
the holds being too full
with bounty from other ports.
The ship sets sail,
the crew joyously heading home.

Near Egypt, the sky started to storm,
the seas started to pitch and boil.
Was it Zeus and Poseidon trading blows?
Or did the sailors forget their offerings?
It matters not, all that matters is the now.
The ship is rocked and tossed,
it is sent up and it is sent down.
It is waved from side to side.
The motion of the ship is so violent
that even the hardiest sailor becomes sick.

Huddled near the main mast,
both merchant and crew find themselves
sick, miserable, and afraid.
Visible is the statue,
the rugs inexplicably gone.
Oh Aphrodite Euploia, Oh Aphrodite Pontia
Save us from the water depths.
We are your children from Naukratis
Oh Aphrodite Eiplimenia
Deliver us safely home!

Before their very eyes,
the ropes become green myrtle,
scenting the air so sweetly
that their stomachs become calm,
as do the raging sea and sky.
As the sun warms their skin,
their spirits do rise
for to home, to loved ones
they would return!

As soon as the ship comes to rest
in their beloved home port,
reverently the Merchant rushes
the savior image and myrtle boughs
to her temple near the docks.
There he gives offerings of thanks
for a safe homecoming,
dedicating the statuette to the temple.

A feast of thanksgiving he then throws
for friends, family, and crew
in the temple of Aphrodite,
giving out the garlands of the sweet myrtle
that adorned the ship
calling them naukratite
and praising Aphrodite's name.

Arrow-Pierced

by Taqerisenu

I am like the silver fish
stranded, caught, gasping,
in the shallow pool.
Love runs out,
with the tide.

No fragile thing, borne
to shore on a clamshell,
pink and frail.
Rather, dark and fathomless,
tasting of salt.

On our bedsheets, still disheveled
like wave-rippled sand,
I spread out in the curves
you left behind,
and dream, arrow-pierced.

Blessings of Aphrodite/Rose Petals
by Pegi Eyers

Atlanta Aphrodite
by Allie Nelson

She puts honey in her hair like it's her wedding
          day
for the bees, for the boys, for her father
all golden and dripping, champagne-sweet
lightning bug lady and queen of June.

They call her Dainty Feet, Sweetheart of Main
          Street
she likes to dance on the village green in choir
          circles
singing "I'm holy, I'm heavenly, I'm his." All the
          men
watch as her ankles move like wind-ripple water.

She ain't dancing for them, though, she dances for
          more
than Man can touch, higher places, where the
          redhawk soars
for she is tall as mountains, summer goddess,
          Elphame Queen.
They ran out of names to call her after a while.

In fever-sweet dreams the boys pray to her, play
          with her
they can never remember the color of her eyes –
if they're blue, hazel, green, or teddy bear brown

but they're shimmering as Kentucky whiskey,
        skipping sun.

The truth is she came to us long ago on moonbeam
        magic
and the gods will take her away just the same, all
        flickering light
bloom of honeysuckle and baby's breath, timbrel of
        angel choir
the Southern Belle tolls, crows fly, the boys
        remember.

Eros Unloosed

by Michael Routery

To primordial Eros, the
First of gods and the fairest, who
With metallic wings outstretched and
Bowstring unloosed, slyly
Trembles mortal and immortal alike
Loose of sense, generating worlds,
Uniting orbs — earth, sun, star and
Moon — and turns the carousel of love,
I raise my cup!

Eternal Aphrodite, Rainbow-Throned

by David W. Landrum

Eternal Aphrodite, rainbow-throned,
You cunning child of Zeus, I pray, I plead:
Don't let the love for which I've wept and groaned
Wither and break me. Come, my prayer heed!

Come down, if ever in my former days
You heard my far-off cries and, hearing, flew,
Leaving the sound of Zeus's golden praise,
Faster than any mortal ever knew.

Swift sparrows, whirring, bore you through the air,
From heaven to darkened earth — then there they
              were!
And you, my blessed lady, kind and fair,
Smiling your immortal smile, asked my desire.

You wondered why I called on you again
And what it was my heart in madness craved:
"Who is it, Sappho? Whom now shall I send?
"Who's wronged you now and made you swear
              and rave?

"If she you love so much has fled away,
"You know that soon she'll be out chasing you!
"And if she scorns your gifts, there'll come the day
"When she will offer gifts to your love due.

"And if she doesn't love you at the first,
"Don't worry! Soon she'll find you're her desire.
"She may not want you now, but soon she'll burst
"And overflow, consumed with passion's fire."

So come to me, and free me! Heed my cry!
From stultifying sorrow, give me aid!
What I am seeking, grant, divine ally.
I wait here in your sacred apple glade.

Here in your temple, smells of frankincense
Mingle with apple blossom. Waters flow,
Cool and refreshing. Roses blossom, dense
And fragrant, and your calming breezes blow.

Here horses, strong with life, do not fear harm
And come to graze. Here drowsy sleep falls
            through
The shimmering leaves. Dear Cypris, pour with
            charm
Your nectar, pure and clear as morning dew,

Into these golden cups. From sacred Crete
Come to me, goddess fair, and let us meet.

Foam-Born

by Jennifer Lawrence

Here in the earliest hours of morning,
  when the birds are still sleeping
  and the beach sands glisten like tiny
  stars under their coating of sea-salt,
Here where the dawn is raw yet,
  naked with possibility,
  pregnant with potential,
You wash ashore like a pearl loosed from its oyster,
  glistening and wet under the newborn
    rays of
  the rising sun, and the fading
  luminescence of the sinking moon.
Here, where graceful seabirds yet slumber,
  unaware of the presence of one
  more beautiful than they, by far,
  birthed out of the opalescent seed
  of castrated Ouranous,
  mingling with the sea's salt,
  flowing forth from the ocean
  whence all life began.

As the sun rises, you unfurl from
sleep, stepping away from the scallop
that bore you to shore; most precious of blossoms,
fair-skinned, gold-tressed, eyes deep and dark
with all the desires contained there
that God or man might feel.

Swans rise in adoring worship and
beat the air with their wings,
joyfully recognizing one whose beauty
makes theirs look like lumps of coal
that look all the more filthy and misshapen
when a diamond gleams among them.

Cytherea, Ourania, Kallipygos,
Cyprian Queen:
we bow before you, stricken mute
by your perfection, and
pray you bless our dull and quiet lives
with the beauty you are known for
and the passion you inspire.
Open our hearts to the love we need
to live, to thrive, to exult in the splendor
of the world around us, and
with your grace fulfill us.

Hail Aphrodite, fierce and gentle lady!
Hail Aphrodite, forgiving and condemning!
Hail Aphrodite, love's queen!

Fox

by Gareth Writer-Davies

you worry
about your (untouched) looks

there is no decay
in the face that might have launched ships

if you
had been arsed to get out of bed

the long epic of immortality
that took

one lover
then another

whilst you lived on
un-changing like the fox that got the goose

Aphrodite
I buckle my hands round your waist

inhale
the wet fur of your pelt

imagine
new ways to kill you

Gifts of Aphrodite

by Amanda Artemisia Forrester

O beautiful Muses Who dance on Helikon Mount
Rich-haired Goddesses Who drink from the
        Hippocrene,
Holy spring of Pegasus, which gives inspiration
Come to me, fair Goddesses, and attend my song.
Sing to me of Golden Aphrodite,
The lovely foam-born Lady
Goddess of Love, Who rules the desires
Of men and beasts alike
She is Primal, Primordial
A force of Nature, unstoppable
Sitting demurely among the Olympian Halls.
O Lady of the Beautiful Tresses,
You are the most powerful on Olympos!
For even the the mind of great Zeus Himself
Must inevitably bend to Your will,
You Who cause sweet love
And maddening desire
To flower in the hearts of all that lives!
How foolish the King of the Gods was
To think that He could harness Your power
By the yoke of marriage to solid Hephaistos!
O Goddess, Your bounty, Your beauty, Your power
Overflows all bounds, like a cup running over
With sweet wine.
May my life always be full of Your radiance
May Your laughter always echo in my ears

May I see Your face in every flower
For Your gifts are more than the ecstasy of sex and
        joy of love
You reign supreme over all the pleasures and joys of
        the world!
Golden-Aphrodite, Laughter-Loving, be near me
        always
And I will sing for You another song.

Goddess

by Beate Sigriddaughter

A woman who is loved
could live forever.

Every moment
a new waterfall, a stone
bridge in the symphony
of canyon wrens,
a kaleidoscope of trust
as strong hands catch
a fearless heart
across the glitter
of our circus tent.

Yes, everything, wild
roses, oh look, another
lizard, goldfinch, hummingbird,
and all the stars outlining
your infinity and mine.

Each morning an anchor
of fire, an angel stretching
to be something more.

My name is Love
and I want to go home.
This shouldn't surprise you,
though perhaps it does.

golden beauty

by Kyler Luffy

a beauty so fierce and blinding,
so soft and alluring

that no man who looks into her
eyes could recapture his heart,

no woman who lay her eye on
such heavenly skin could
again feel warmth on her own,

not one who witnesses the light
of her beauty could ever again
muster the strength,
or the will,
to walk away from such
warmth, such
soothing sweetness.

her presence is like the lick
of a flame,

hot on the skin but
warm to the soul,

her voice like honey,
sweet and thick.

and I think her hands must be
stained bright ruby,
covered in the life of those
whose hearts she mangled
in revenge for ignorance;

vengeance hot on her tongue as
she closes the eyes
of those who still revel in her
golden beauty.

the heart leads men to their
ends,
passion leads men to life,
what —
beside love,
beside passion,
could drive one to spill their
own blood?

such sweet warmth, such ethereal
beauty could drive a man mad;
she will tell you,
it would be wiser to turn away,
close your eyes and dream of
darkness.

because the light on her skin
will haunt you,
your eyes will see her glow cast
upon everything,

and you will be lost to a
passion that consumes and
devours,
and you will still long to hear
her honeyed-tongue whisper to
you once again.

The Golden Ladies of Love

by Amanda Artemisia Forrester

I sing my song of the Golden Ladies of both lands
Aphrodite and Hathor, the laughter-loving
Goddesses of love
Who some say are the same Being
Perhaps They are, or perhaps not
They may be Divine sisters, or cousins in the starry
      firmament
But in truth it matters not.
Aphrodite I sing first, for I have known Her longest
The curly-haired match-maker of Grecian lands
Who delights in flowers and the songs of lovers
Beautiful is She, but not weak
For nothing is stronger
      — Nor fiercer —
Then true love.
The slim-ankled Kypress-born Lady loves Ares,
The rough-handed soldier's God.
She dons bronze armor and hefts a spear
To follow Him into battle
Aphrodite fights like a wild animal
To protect Her love.
Beautiful Aphrodite is not a delicate thing
She does not shudder at the thought of conflict.

Lady Hathor, cow-formed Goddess of Aiegyptos,
I sing to You as well. Lover of Horus the strong-
      armed

Lady of Drunkenness Who dances in the temple
        precinct,
I have not known You for long,
Yet You already have captured my heart.
Your large cow-eyes express every emotion that
        plays in Your heart
And despite Your carefully coiffed beauty
You do not hesitate to laugh loudly from deep in
        Your belly.
Your form is full and womanly
All soft curves, heavy breasts and wide hips
No anorexic sprite are You!
For You delight in all the pleasures life has to offer
The fullness of sex, food, love, beer, and dance.
May I dance for You, Goddess,
And shake the sistrum in Your honor
As Your priestesses of old once did
In the stone temples of the Egyptian desert.

Hail to You both, the Golden Ladies of Greece and
        Egypt
Goddesses of all pleasures and joys of corporeal
        existence
Divine Sisters of love, sheathed in linen under the
        desert sun.
I offer You my heart in all its rawness
May I always be blessed with the grace of Your
        Presences,
With the courage to own my desires,
Love for all the world
And love for my own self and body.

Let me remember
That my spirit resides in my body
And I must nurture both.

A Grammar for Aphrodite

by Michael Routery

O foam-born one, rising wet from the wave,
Paphian Aphrodite passing high in the sky,
bursting with love, pulled in chariot by twittering
birds, heads cocked above the clouds, listening
for your worshipper's desires. Laughter loving
Aphrodite, you appear in the most
surprising places. Yes,
let us talk about the things of love,
the toys of erotic play, let's Aphrodite,
as you are noun, verb, conjunction
and interjection, perfumed one of the copula,
connoisseur of lovers of all assortments,
expert at conjoining in your gardens
of lust, delighting in metaphor, Eros by your side,
most ancient goddess.

Hermes' and Aphrodite's Child

by Michael Routery

I gather a bouquet for Hermaphroditus,
you of the graceful curves and plentitude of shape,
uniting genders in your sumptuous body,
offering a harvest of interpretations.
Though some see you as frail
(even if offering healing) I do not, and am not so
        sure
about fawn-skinned Salmacis the nymph
being once engrafted onto your boy's body either,
as Ovid claimed, but I do know you are the child
of Hermes, most knowledgeable, and Aphrodite,
most beautiful, and sibling of Priapus, the over-
        burdened.
Indolent and luxurious as the magnolia blossom,
as glossy as its leaves, redolent as an orchid
in a crystal pavilion, you lie waiting, pheromones
        wafting
for the soft-winged pollinators of double love's
        night ....

Hymn and Invocation of Aphrodite

by Apollonius Sophistes
(John Opsopaus)

Oh Muse! With visions Thou hast filled my soul,
with visions overpowering, for Thou
hast shown me Golden Aphrodite! Now
the blaze emboldens me; like coal
to brighter burning fanned by Breath Divine,
the Cyprian enflameth me with words,
seductive sounds, which swiftly would entwine
my soul, as lime-twigs trap unwary birds.

An ancient poet[1] spake the truth; he said:
When Cypris cometh swift, high-spirited
just like a Hero — irresistible
Her onslaught, nor may anyone annul
Her summons; flouting Her is arrogance,
a failure to respect the difference
'tween Gods and Mortals; nor can even They
resist Her Power. She is held at bay
by only three: Athena, Bright-Eyed Maid,
and Artemis, who haunts both wood and glade,
and Hestia reject the Paphian's Dove,
for They alone deny delights of Love.
The Cyprian's summons is a challenge. Be
thou brave and answer it, for verily
a God hath willed it; surely stinging grief
will be refusal's price, so seek relief,
conforming to the Paphian's Will.

Thus spake the Poet truths he would instill.
Far-shining Aphrodite, hear our prayer!
Thou Laughter-loving Lady, Paphian,
Well-girded, Golden, Sea-born, Cyprian,
Companion, Tender-hearted, or howe'er
it pleaseth Thee to be addressed, attend,
we ask, our words of praise, and send
Thy Grace, because Thou art the source of all
that's charming, graceful, all that doth enthrall
in word or deed, in action, figure, face.
For Thine is the allure that doth enlace
our hearts as one, for as the charmed is bound,
so also is the charmer quickly found
surrendering, with yearning undisguised,
the compromiser gladly compromised!
But irresistible is even this:
seducer falling to seduction; bliss
repaid is twofold bliss, drawing tight
the bonds about them both, in shared delight.

❤

Now I call in ancient sounds:
Ἀφροδίτη Χρυσοστέφανε Γλυκυμείλιχ᾽ Ὁ ἦ
Καλλίγλουτε Θεὰ πάνδημε Ἑταίρα σὺ Μορφώ,[2]

❤

Or whatever name doth please Thee,
hear! If ever I've appeased Thee,
now attend my prayer beseeching,

see my hands toward Thee reaching,
know my love is everlasting!
Lady, grant the gift I'm asking
and appear before us, whether
now sojourning deep in Nether
Regions with the Queen of Hades,
or in Heaven with Thy Ladies,
founts of all allure, the Graces,
fair Their form and fair Their faces!

I request Thee, leave Thy station!
Grant to us a visitation!
Show to us Thy face delightful!
Let us worship Thee as rightful,
shapely form that's Thine adoring!
Hear our voices now upsoaring
to the Heavens from our chorus!
Please, we ask Thee, stand before us!

Queen of Twilight, Queen of Morning!
Deeds just done or now aborning
are Thy favorites; prized the clever
warrior of the bold endeavor!
Dear to Thee the Sun that's rising,
Thou reward for enterprising
souls, Thou prize for tasks completed,
Thou in rivalry entreated
to bestow Thy grace, advising,
bold advances galvanizing!
Such Thy gift and such Thy favor,
bounty for the bolder, braver!

Source of charm in words and faces,
propagating species, races,
with desire their hearts entwining,
Thou in starry splendor shining,
Aphrodite, hear us calling!
Show to us Thy form enthralling!

Golden Goddess, we beseech Thee,
stretch our arms, and long to reach Thee!
Shining Star of Heaven, hear us!
We implore Thee, come Thou near us!

Hear our holy hymn rejoicing
and Thy praises loudly voicing!
Shining Star of Heaven, hear us!
We beseech Thee, come Thou near us!

See our faces t'ward Thee turning!
Feel the flames within us burning!
Shining Star of Heaven, hear us!
We beseech Thee, come Thou near us!

Show Thy features! Hold us Spellbound!
Come Thou Lady, Goddess, Gold-crowned,
Merciful and Mighty,
Laughter-loving Aphrodite!

A shining star! It's streaking through the skies,
descending earthward, dazzling to my eyes.

A vision riseth, showing through the glare,
a scene of beauty, overwhelming, rare.
I see Her temple standing by the shore
of Cypris, glistening marble walls and floor
reflected in the rippling water, stark
against the sacred grove's deep green, and dark
the columns flanking there the open door,
through which, in the serene interior,
I see Her Holy Harlots, standing there,
devoted to their Goddess, eagerly to share
the Gifts of Aphrodite. There's no shame
to sharing Love's embraces in Her name.

Below the sea appeareth now a light
that gloweth green, as when a candle bright
behind an emerald burns. The sea is churned
with froth and foam; a figure is discerned
arising from the depths, a Form Divine,
the Cyprian, approaching on the brine.
She cometh quickly, skimming over wave
and water; such a scene we would engrave
upon our hearts forever. Steppeth She
from off the cockle shell. Our earnest plea
was heard! Now look upon the Golden One,
attractiveness without comparison
is Hers; embodied beauty is Her gift,
whatever form doth most the heart uplift.

O gracious Muse, bestow on me, I pray,
the words to do Her justice, nor betray
the Goddess of all Beauty, Charm and Grace,

whate'er attracts in action, word, or face!

Before us, confident in Her control,
She standeth proudly, bright eyes piercing, soul
enflaming, nor denying Her allure,
in Works of Love unbashful and secure.
Our admiration's obvious; a smile
doth part Her lips, and turneth She awhile
before our gaze — but slippeth now Her gown,
the strap upon Her shoulder falling down
so naked now from nape to arm we see
the swelling of Her chest, that like the sea
doth rise and fall in measured rate,
and both the heart and eyes doth captivate.

As She approacheth with a careful stride
I see a tremor that doth coincide
with ev'ry step, beneath Her gossamer
attire, a motion unmistakable,
a lure She knows is inescapable.

The Paphian, stopping in our steady gaze,
with insolent eyes accepteth all our praise.
Her hip out-thrust, She standeth there,
Her brazen posture an unspoken dare
to us. I watch Her naked arm draw back
the folds, exposing bare Her side, no lack
of satin skin to see, so taut around
Her hip; transfixed by this, I'm held spell-bound.

Far more than mortal eyes can comprehend
are sights like these I see. A friend
indeed is Aphrodite, showing us
embodied beauty, a gift most generous.

A drifting cloud now comes across the scene;
the vision fades, dissolving into mist.
But though the Goddess can't be seen,
we feel Her presence; having once been kissed
by Her and gazed in rapture at Her face,
we know the worth of Elegance and Grace,
nor ever will forget it; t'ward Beauty too
we're urged, and Joy that doth the Soul renew.

We thank Thee Goddess for Thy welcome gifts,
for pleasures and delights, all that lifts
us up to Ecstasy, for they are Thine.
We pray Thy liberal Love may always shine
on us, may always rouse our spirits, spur
us on to seek whatever's lovelier.

And if my poem hath appealed to Thee,
I pray that kindly wouldst Thou look on me.

Notes

The foregoing was inspired by a vision of the
Goddess; it is dedicated to Aphrodite and may be
used for any nonprofit purpose, provided that credit
is given. It is a revision of a poem originally

published in *Green Egg*, Vol. 28, No. 109 (Summer 1995), pp. 32–33. © 1993, John Opsopaus.

1 — Euripedes, *Hippolytus*: 443, 474.

2 — That is, *Aphrodítê Khrûsostéphane Glukumeílikh' Ô hê / Kallígloute Theà Pándême Hetaíra sù Morphô*, which means "Aphrodite Gold-crowned Sweetly-winning O (Thou) the / Beautiful-butt Goddess Of-all-people Courtesan Thou Shapely-one" — all ancient epithets of Aphrodite.

Ancient Greek pronunciation guidelines: If unaccented syllables are the tonic (say, C) then the acute accent is a rising fifth (C-G), the grave accent is a falling third (G-E), and the circumflex accent is a rising-falling fifth (C-G-C). Vowels should be pronounced as in Italian; ê denotes long e ("ay"); û is like a German ü, ô is a long o. The tonal intervals are approximate, and would be less in everyday speech. The combinations kh, ph and th should be pronounced as aspirated k, p, and t, respectively. Trill the "r"s.

Aphrodite Calls to Pele
by Laurie Goodhart

Hymn to Aphrodite

by Leni Hester

From the starry vault of heaven,
O Divine and Radiant One,
I call you.

From the foam-lapped shores of the wine-dark sea,
O Gracious and Beloved,
I call you.

Aphrodite, daughter of the stars, of the sea, mother
   of muses, of grace and harmony,
She who creates all beautiful things of flesh and
   spirit,
O Divine One,
I call to you.

Rising from the ocean swell, clothed in golden
   brace and green sea pearl,
You dwell in the spiral coil of the rose, in the dew
   upon the poppy and the apple bloom,
while doves call in the pine, the swan and cob
   glide through dawn mist.

The world is bathed in your radiant light,
O Golden One,
who engenders every work of art and craft,
who brings beauty and shameless abundance
wherever you go.

Glorious One, who unites the world in bonds of
        love and desire,
I call you.

I sing the praise of the source of unending Love in
        the midst of violence,
and ask for the blessings of your heart: courage, joy,
        compassion, desire,
passion, service, reverence and lust — all these and
        more do I ask and offer you,
O Queen,
O Mystery,
O Soul of Nature that gives life to the Universe.
All that lives is the proof of your love

I Am Isis-Aphrodite, Goddess of the Deep Blue Sea

by Chelsea Luellon Bolton

I am the Goddess of the maritime sea.
I am Isis-Aphrodite.
I am the Goddess of the Stars above,
I am the Goddess of Love.
I am the Goddess of the deep, blue sea.
All will surrender to Me.
I am the Goddess of the Winds that blow,
I am the Goddess of the Earth below.
I am the Goddess of Winds and Tides,
I am the Goddess Who never hides.
I am a lover and a wife.
I am not a Goddess of trysts.
Adonis,
Osiris,
and Sarapis, too:
These are the Gods whom I woo.
I am the Goddess of Gales,
I am the Goddess of Sails.
Ships carry My name.
I am a Goddess ever-famed.
For protection and care,
I am always there.
I weep and search for My slain love.
My tears flow from above.
I weep and wail
But to no avail.

Both the sea and storm, swell;
I am the Goddess of this as well.
My tears flow as rain
this expresses My pain.
I am the Goddess of the mourning shroud,
I shriek very loud.
I keen, I mourn, I take a breath.
I lay My love down to rest.
One tear slips and then I see
The White flower changes before Me.
The rose once white as the tops of the waves
Becomes a hue darker, a red rose I've made.
I lay them upon His grave.
I am a Goddess of the mourning shroud,
I am the Goddess who keens very loud.
I am the Goddess of the Congenial Bed.
I've strewn the roses upon it — My husband is dead.
I am the Goddess of the Bridal Bed.
I am the Goddess of those who have Wed.
For those Who seek Wedded Bliss,
Do not ask Me for this.
I am a Widow, once a Wife,
This is My life.
I place a red rose on their graves,
I weep as a maid.
Osiris of the Grain and Adonis of the Flower,
I weep every hour.
My tears bring plants life,
I am no longer a wife.
I am the Goddess of Gardens and Gales,
I am the Goddess Who Wails.

I am the Goddess of the Red thorned flower,
I am the Goddess of the life power.
I bring life from death,
I lay Him down to rest.
I weep, I mourn, I keen a song that shatters glass,
I am the Goddess Who knows what will come
to pass.
I am the Black Robed Goddess with a veil.
I am the Goddess holding a sail.
I am the Goddess of ships, ports and harbors, too.
I am the Goddess Who will always answer you.
I am the Goddess of the deep, blue sea.
How would you know Me?
I am the Goddess of the Wind and Rain,
I am the Goddess ever-famed.
I am the Goddess with the sea-green eyes,
I am the Goddess of the roaring tides.
I am the Goddess of Winds that blow
What more would you know?
I am the Goddess of ships, traders and merchants,
too.
Yes, even you.
I am the Goddess of the deep, blue sea.
I aid those who call upon Me.
I am the Goddess who guides the waves,
I am the Goddess of the graves.
I am the Goddess who lights the way,
I am one whose magic is in what I say.
I shall not stray from My path.
All you need do is ask.
In darkness, I lead through dim-lit harbors,

With the bright light I guide
through the waves and tides.
I am the Goddess of sea-green eyes,
I am the Lady of the roaring tides.
I am the Goddess of Heaven as well,
I am the Goddess who makes rivers and oceans
        swell.
I am the Goddess Shining Bright
as the Golden One and the Star at Night
I am the Goddess of the Morning Star
I shine wherever you are.
I am the Goddess of the Heavenly sphere,
I am the Goddess, Ever-Near.
Venus is My star at night and in the morn,
You will never be forlorn.
I am the Goddess of Wind and Rain,
I am the Goddess ever-famed.
For Her feats in love and valor.
I am the Goddess of the hour.
I am the Goddess of Wisdom and War.
I am the Goddess of the Oar.
I am the Goddess of Wind and Sea.
It is impossible to miss Me.
I am the Goddess of Storms and Strife.
I am a Goddess Who was a Wife.
I am a Goddess of Winds and Gales,
Forever Shall I Sail.
On the deep, blue sea.
Everyone can see Me,
in the waves and tides.
I am always by Your side.

La Primavera

by Mary Geschwindt

I am born of the immortal image of beauty.
Aglaea and Euphrosyne and Thalia,
Ethereal Graces dance before Botticelli's vision.
The time for charity ceases abruptly
As cast in vices —
Just as once ideals were cast in shimmering gold
        and bronze —
Is the dawn of an ephemeral race.
The winds bring on the epoch of change
As Zephyrus seeks new follies and
Transforms a childlike wonder into
The Bearer of Life.

Centuries from now you will know those fruitless
        words,
The ardent motif with which I infect
The soul of John Keats, Poet Emeritus:
"Beauty is truth, truth beauty."
You feed off truth in the quest for eternal glory.
I know eternity like no other man
Nor God could care to wish.
Divinity blinds you,
And you will never understand truth —
Not until you accept the blind eyes, the coarse
        hands,
And repent for your barren devotions.
Cupid's cruel arrow instills in you

A hardened love.

One day you will forget me,
Yearning and careening like little devils.
I am the elegy. I am the dream.
Still you fail each day to recognize
A distinct schism in reality.
You are the only reality
Wandering in the only dream!
I live in the garden. I live in the springtime.
You work hard all winter,
Consumed by dirt. The end of the living,
Sacrificing and devouring, wasting time.

I watch you with sanguine eyes
As you excavate earth.
If only you had lifted your eyes instead of shovels
And taken at once the hand I hold before you,
You would have the key to Paradise
At your unforgiving fingertips.
Flora and Fauna flourishing
Before the common man.
That is Heaven on earth.
Build the steps to Paradise,
Scatter the roses and thorns in the throne room,
And receive the crown.

The day will come when
Over worn with sweaty vehemence
A spark ignites the fire and
Burns the garden to ash.

I will begin anew while
Men die and fade away,
Breaking with the entropy of civilization —
Demons and Deities are forever.
To you who hold life and death in your grasp
         without knowing,
This is beauty — absolute beauty,
This is the truth.

Digging, digging, digging in my flowerbeds all the
         while,
You uncovered the tomb and saw
What was not there.
Empty all this time!
As I have stood unmoving
In your mortal picture, over mortal centuries,
I will not turn from you now,
But resolve to keep watch forever,
For as long as you intend to endeavor.

Love and Commitment

by Merit Brokaw

I used to believe
love is all in a relationship
everything else would follow
naturally in succession
I want to believe
part me fights to believe
how foolish
how naive
how childish
Glorious Aphrodite's gifts
catalysts for a relationship
respect, like, lust, love, need
relationship roots, these are
non-sustaining on their own
survival beyond
sunny days of laughter
through the rain of tears
through dark nights of uncertainty
through torments of jealousy, anger
takes commitment
Aphrodite's emotional package
her hormonal urges
are a house of cards on their own
another is required for a solid frame
one known for her patience,
her commitment in good times and bad
Passionate, Determined Hera

All the love in the world
contained within one relationship
will wither and die
when the excitement is gone
when the newness wears off
weeks, months, years can go by
yet if commitment isn't there
neither will the relationship
only a farce that disappears
in the gentlest of breezes

Jealous Hera
terrible the acts
of a jealous heart
jealousy is a warning
lines are down, no dial tone
prompt resolution
tools of patience and compromise
nasty necessary compromises
leaving all pleased, all disappointed
yet the sign of commitment
requires a bit selflessness
as the selfish are committed
only to themselves

Hail Aphrodite!
May your gifts keep the heart pumping!
Hail Hera!
May your gifts be the glue
that keeps it strong and healthy!

One

by Terence Kuch

Count all my loves?
Can you number
the leaves on the trees
or waves of the sea?

But I, in Eros' laughing
grasp, I count each lover
"One!"

Piercer of Souls

by Rodopi Sisamis

In the heart of disappointment, I find you.

I have had this dream before.
"Watch how she'll fall," you say triumphantly, as
the other goddesses crowd around.
You are full of color and life, next to you, they fade
       like ghosts.
I wear your colors,
I have always worn them,
although sometimes beneath my skin, hidden where
I could not tear
       them off.

When others say,
I'm a lover not a fighter
I laugh, in that same cold way as you.
Anyone who knows you, knows that to love is a
fight to the death.

"You have to want it," you whisper in my ear.
"You can't have it, if you don't want it."

Love is not the eating of the heart,
Endless nights of hunger and madness, as I gnaw at
       my own flesh.
Aberrations that amuse you,
The pleasure in the darkness:

That realm is also yours.

The lessons that you teach me,
The roses inked into my skin,
all the way down into the meat;
The meaning woven into my name:

Oh mother, cruel and beautiful mother,
You are merciless to the foolish,
An exposed blade to those who lack the courage
To swim in your waters.

But in your wisdom,
In your harsh lessons,
We find the gods within.

Where Eros' arrows are lodged in our hearts,
There you enter and do your work.

Prayer to Aphrodite II

by Rebecca Buchanan

Aphrodite
Crowned with roses
Sweet smile
Axe and whip in hand
to cleave the heart
and sting the tongue

— teach me to play

Primal Made Flesh

by Merit Brokaw

Helen, Sex incarnate.
Mortal surrogate of Aphrodite.
Pity Paris. Pity the Prince of Troy.
When caught between three,
he chose one and got two,
for wherever the surrogate goes,
soon her lady will follow.
Aphrodite, primal goddess,
born from castration,
wild in all senses of the word.
Helen brought that wildness
to the beds of king and prince.
Destruction was inevitable.
Love is a force of nature
that invades and controls.
It can build one up or
tear one down.
Usually it does both
catching the interest of Nemesis
who takes down the arrogant.
Better for Paris to have bathed
in Selemnos to cure his affliction
than consort in the bed
of Aphrodite's shining one.

Sappho and the Woman of Starlight

by John W. Sexton

> ἦρος ἄγγελος ἱμερόφωνος ἀήδων
> *Nightingale, you sing desire;*
> *you are Spring's harbinger, crier. (Sappho)*

A clot of birds appears in the pure sky.
Hidden in that shifting cloud of sparrows
is seated Aphrodite,
come through all the night and into the day
from the far Pleiades.

She knows this, for on the previous midnight,
as Pleiades set with the moon,
she saw a splinter fall from one of the stars.

The sparrows separate just above the field
and Sappho averts her gaze. The dark, compact
bodies of the sparrows were shielding a woman
of glaring silver. She shines, not with the sunlight
of day, but with a light more ancient,
a light from a greater distance, a light
of both the past and the future, a light
unstopping and unstoppable, regardless of day or
        night.

The light now is in her mind, and the light
is thought. *Daughter, you will have the language*
of starlight, incorruptible through all the ages.

Long after your pages have rotted, your words
will continue on. Write, daughter, of the world you
        know,
of the things you see; and between those words
will be the things unknown, the things invisible.
Write, daughter, and out-write the words of men.

Then the voice is gone from her mind and the light
is gone from the field. The sparrows chirp from the
        hedges
and all that is left is sunlight.

But in her mind, and in her verses yet to come,
is unstoppable starlight. Starlight that has travelled
        long
and will travel yet, regardless of day or night.

Sonnet for Aphrodite

by David Subacchi

Your beauty so worried the gods on Olympus
That Zeus and Hera married you to their son
Hephaestus, the ugly, wretched and deformed one,
To avoid war over the spawn of Uranus
For possession of a body so marvelous.
Overjoyed he loved you with passion tremendous
Forging with twisted hands fine trinkets of iron
To adorn your graceful form before everyone
Further augmenting an attraction dangerous.

But for his loyalty you found so little use
Labouring in vain before anvil and furnace,
That bored with such plainness you soon played fast
        and loose
With many gods and men and with your Adonis.
Goddess of love that treated your spouse with abuse
Searching for attraction in every pretty face.

Aphrodite as the Red Baroness
by Ravenart

To Aphrodite by the Muses
(Red Baroness is she of the sacred hive)

by Ravenart

Holy holy holy is the Lady Aphrodite divine
Daughter is she of starry sperm and of salty womb
　　　darkly mirror'd
Blessed be she, the beguiler and the strifer beyond
　　　time
In her, worlds full of dangerous grace bloom'd
In her, man raise his city tall and fair-align'd
Behold the whole earth is full of her glory untimed
Gamekeeper of evolution's arena enshired
Tame blacksmith's heart she eschew
The insolent killer's heart in she exude
The deadly strife of pleasure be fine
To lay low the established customs untimed
On the bloodland of many invisible hosts be the
　　　cunts bedew'd
To erect the fresh power of the day
Holy holy holy is the Lady Aphrodite divine
Daughter is she of starry sperm and of salty womb
darkly mirror'd
Blessed be she, the beguiler and the strifer beyond
　　　time
In her, worlds full of dangerous grace bloom'd
In her, man raise his city tall and fair-align'd
Red Baroness is she of the sacred hive
Grantor of apple golden, waker of marble formed
　　　fine

Heartbreak her spur to greater mastery, O truly
Lo, the bold and the charmer find their ally
Lo, the slacker and the graceless find their scourge
        assign'd
In her war fathered beauty and grace divine
By her fire sacred the old growth burnt tartly
And midwifing the fresh valley
By her will, to adventuresome enslavement a maid
        incline
By her will, an assassin beloved scale forbidden
        tower moonshined
The former strength of men seized by passion
        newfoundly
Restore them body and soul as she may coyly
And raise high the glittering standard of the arts
        design'd.

To Begin

by Alexeigynaix

red roses bloom in a clear vase
an offering to the Blossoming One
to the Ally in Love and War

I want to honor Her
but I hardly know where to start

so I begin with an impulse buy
a dozen roses from the grocery store

perhaps next I will speak of the Night-Black One
the Golden One, wife to the Bronzesmith
perhaps next I will fashion bronze trinkets
as He might to please Her
perhaps next I will condense my thoughts
into a piece of poetic art —

I want to honor Her
but I do not know Her
only what others say of Her

so I'll display those roses
a stick of frankincense I'll light
I'll speak hymns others wrote about Her
at lovely people I'll smile bright

and one of these days I'll find
better words to tell Her
what is in my heart

Tributary

by Richard King Perkins

How can you not be captivated
by her Grecian chic
and delicate bare feet,
singing with sounds
borrowed from anemone
and deepest sea foam.
She is offering new branches —
divergent histories
and celestial caresses.
Kneel with her a moment,
let her lips press your human vestiges
and her hands remove
stain and defeat from your permanence.
You bathe in wet earth,
unbecoming yourself
spilling the last illness
into her forgiving lap.
Now try to look at her once more.
Her clothing conceals nothing.
Her feet glide over intangible soil.

Venus

by Merit Brokaw

sex and love
beauty and enticement
seduction and persuasion
victory and wine
these are your gifts

Lady of Myrtles
your devotees seek you
out of desire, not obligation
they seek your favor, your grace
your charm, your *je ne sais quoi*
for you temper the fiery
uniting opposites in affection
whether divine or mortal

Lady of Roses
yours is the wedding night
no care in you for the contract
yet your flowers adorn
the bride's bouquet
your image rightfully placed
on her household shrine

Mother of Rome
whose temple was placed
upon their Capitoline Hill
granting political favors

and military victories
bearing the triumphant laurel

Lady of Wine
your drink graces the table
of the everyday life
of both common and elite
for your abundant blessings
enable gardens and vineyards
to produce that which feeds
both body and soul

Hail gracious goddess
may you be pleased
with this prose
and bless my life
with your pleasant gifts.

Venus

by Ashley Dioses

An evening star or morning's shine,
In love and hope, this realm is mine.
Such lust and beauty sets a fire,
Romance creates a hot desire.
My harmony sheds light on all,
Just come to me and heed my call.

Venus and Felix Roma

by Michael Routery

Hadrian set Venus to face the bloody
Coliseum, reinscribing martial Rome with amor,
Which, as the emperor via his temple
Architecturally ordained, is Roma backwards.
The temple where the two goddesses sat back to
       back
Was built on the site of Nero's
Golden House and leaden crimes.
The shimmering green goddess,
The alluring one, cast her spell upon the city,
Backed by her sister; the cavalcade of history
Broke over the metropolis — churches and columns
Commingled, promiscuous in baroque subversions,
Bedecking a city no longer of empire but
Of *La dolce vita*, Fellini's carnival.
O Venus Felix, your power, your seduction
Still washes over the city in perfumed waves,
Spins desire in elegance and glamour,
From the Spanish Steps to the Pincio, from
Santa Francesca Romana* to Castel Sant' Angelo.

*[Author's Note: The church of Santa Francesca
Romana was built on the site of the temple.]*

Venus Victrix

by Taqerisenu

It comes softly,
sweeping over
like a wave,
gentleness belying —

And I am under
Her,
pinned, like a specimen
for dissection.

Scientists cannot quantify,
oyster shell ribcage cracked open
wide,
searching for pearls.
No armor can resist
Her
sword pressed, sharply sweet,
at the breast.

It comes fiercely,
pulling from beneath
like undertow,
cruelty belying —

How sweet surrender is,
like the taste of an apple.

Where Does Love Go When It's Cold?
by Lori Anne Gravley

*[After "Venus Frigida" by Peter Paul Rubens
(1614)]*

Huddled in a cave under the watch
of goats and boys, both *flagrante*

so that you turn your head away
though the blond hair that covers your breasts

is surely more temptation than shield —
the red cloak before a bull in Pamplona

and it's red you're resting on and red
the fire somewhere reflected in your skin

though too far to warm you. Are you even tempted
by all that fur and the warmth of that animal

body or do you see the child huddled, maybe
            sleeping
as deterrent? Is that the sun

setting in the distance or is it rising?

Winged Lover

by Deborah Guzzi

[After: *Favorite Greek Myths* by Mary Pope
Osborne, "Psyche and Cupid" with artist-illustrator
Troy Howell.]

As flies to wanton boys are we to th'gods,
Shakespeare — *King Lear* Act 4, scene 1, 32-37

In kindness, Cupid's scratch was not foresworn,
within the plane of Psyche's aura love crested.
The bitter tears he replaced with joy reborn.
Now, upward she would rise and there be tested,
unknown to him his kindness she contested.

How was this kind, she could not see his form,
yet felt his hand, his weight, the space he nested?
Yet, he feared for her, feared his mother's scorn,
feared the lash's fall, from not doing as requested.
Oh but, Psyche's human loveliness was blessed.

In kindness, Cupid hid Psyche from the storm
but with curiosity she was infested;
sore wounded was her love, he left forlorn,
hurt; she had not conformed as he requested.
Many trials she met and passed though tested.

When kindness by curiosity is deformed,
trials and tribulations must be suggested

for God's jealousy is not easily born
and lessons too easily given can be bested
so harshness, not kindness, was invested.

Essays

Aphrodite Ἀφρογένεια (Foam-Born)
by Devon Power

Aphrodite and Theology

by Edward P. Butler

Children, the Cyprian is not the Cyprian alone, but she is called by many names. She is Hades, she is immortal life, she is raving madness, she is unmixed desire, she is lamentation; in her is all activity, all tranquillity, all that leads to violence. For she sinks into the vitals of all that have life; who is not greedy for that Goddess? She enters into the swimming race of fishes, she is within the four-legged brood upon dry land, and her wing ranges among birds ... among beasts, among mortals, among the race of Gods above. Which among the Gods does she not wrestle and throw three times? If I may speak out — and I may speak out — to tell the truth, she rules over the heart of Zeus, without spear, without iron. All the plans of mortals and of Gods are cut short by the Cyprian — Sophocles frag. 941 (trans. Hugh Lloyd-Jones).

The holy heaven yearns to wound the earth, and yearning layeth hold on the earth to join in wedlock; the rain, fallen from the amorous heaven, impregnates the earth, and it bringeth forth for mankind the food of flocks and herds and Demeter's gifts; and from that moist marriage-rite the woods put on their bloom. Of all these things I am the cause — Aphrodite, frag. 25 of Aeschylus' *Danaïdes* (trans. Herbert Weir Smyth).

She came forth, a reverend, beautiful Goddess, and grass grew up around her beneath her slender feet. Gods and men call her 'Aphrodite', the foam-born Goddess — Hesiod, *Theogony* 194-6 (trans. Glenn W. Most).

Aphrodite, according to Hesiod, is the most senior of the Olympians. Indeed, Aphrodite belongs properly to the generation of the Titans, as 'daughter' of Ouranos by way of Pontus, the sea; hence among her popular epithets is *Pontia*.[1] When Kronos has cut off the genitals of Ouranos, he throws them into the sea, where "they were borne along the water for a long time, and a white foam [*aphros*] rose up around them from the immortal flesh; and inside this grew a maiden," (*Theogony*, 189-192, trans. Most). The Ouranian genitalia has been in this way 'cut off', that is, isolated from the ordinary reproductive cycle to function in a different fashion and on a wider cosmic plane. One may focus on the violence of this act, as Hesiod clearly does, and which is expressed concretely in the beings who come forth from the blood spilled on the Earth thereby, namely the Erinyes, the

---

[1] On Aphrodite's maritime associations, see Denise Demetriou, "*Tês pasês nautiliês phulax*: Aphrodite and the Sea," *Kernos* 23 (2010), pp. 67-89.

Giants, and the Melian Nymphs,[2] but the mytheme also invites comparison to the Egyptian Heliopolitan cosmogony, in which Atum's primordial act of masturbation similarly releases his seed into a watery abyss where it takes form for itself. In the Heliopolitan myth, the orgasmic moment is separated off as directly productive, without the need for a full generative partner, only the waters as a passive receptacle, while Atum's hand, personified as the Goddess Iusâas, plays an intermediary role in some versions. The Hesiodic myth, as different as it is, performs nevertheless an analogous symbolic isolation of the phallus, which, moreover, as separated from the reproductive economy, is no longer meaningfully 'male' as opposed to 'female'.[3]

---

[2] The Melian Nymphs are the mothers of the humans of the warlike 'Bronze Age' (*Works and Days* 143ff), the ash trees with which they are associated providing the wood for spears. On the Erinyes, note that Hesychius mentions 'Erinye' as an epithet of Aphrodite (Gabrielle Pironti, *Entre ciel et guerre: Figures d'Aphrodite en Grèce ancienne* (Liège: Presses universitaires de Liège, 2007), chap. 1, §137), and a fragment of Epimenides (DK 3 B19) makes out Aphrodite, the Fates and the Erinyes all to be daughters of Kronos (Pironti chap. 1, §155). [All references to Pironti are by chapter and paragraph number in the electronic edition.]

[3] Recall, in this respect, Aphrodite's power to change the sex of Leukippos of Phaistos (Antoninus Liberalis, *Metamorphoses* 17; Nicander, *Heteroioumena* frag. 45 Schneider), or of the goat Theseus is about to sacrifice before he takes to sea (Plutarch, *Theseus* 18.3; Pironti, chap. 3, §94, 99).

This raises the issue of the role played by Eros in the stages of the theogony prior to Aphrodite's emergence. Once Aphrodite has emerged, Hesiod says that "with her went Eros" (201). Eros becomes subordinate to Aphrodite henceforth, to the degree that in later antiquity the image arises of Eros as her infant son. But for Hesiod, Eros is one of the very first Gods to come forth into the cosmos. From out of Chaos — which is probably to be understood, in accord with the most likely etymology, from *chaunos*, porous, spongy, hence neither solid nor void — emerges at once Earth (Gaia), the solid; Tartaros, the void; and Eros. The sense of the primordial chaos as *chaunos* is echoed in the etymologizing of the name 'Aphrodite' from *aphros*, 'foam', from the foamy quality shared by semen and by seawater, foam being a mixture of liquid and void as the spongy or porous is of solid and void.[4] Eros is the principle of production for the generations to come until Aphrodite takes over the task. Then Eros will be, so to speak, born again to Aphrodite and Ares, placing him firmly within the social realm. The reproductive function as administered by proto-cosmic Eros, by contrast, seems analogous to budding. It is, at any rate, a mode of (re)production

---

[4] Diogenes of Apollonia theorized that semen is formed from blood when it becomes frothy (*aphrôdes*) (64B6 Diels-Kranz). (Pironti, chap. 3, §21.)

which does not involve intersubjectivity, a relationship between persons *as* persons.

The first step in a movement beyond primordial Eros comes when Gaia brings forth from herself Ouranos, the heavens. He is her product, and yet Hesiod stresses that he is "equal to herself" (126). Gaia and Ouranos are the first Gods to have a relationship, but they lack a mediating agency, a space of encounter, of simultaneous presence to and distance from one another, *between* them. Hence Gaia's children by Ouranos, the Titans, are conceived one after another and yet unable to be truly born. There is no space for them to distinguish themselves, and so they remain suspended as dependents of the relationship between Gaia and Ouranos. This situation, however, causes Gaia discomfort such that she solicits the assistance of her youngest, Kronos, to castrate his father with a sickle of flint. A place must be opened for the emergence of the children of Gaia and Ouranos by interrupting the cycle of Ouranos begetting children upon her without it making a *difference*. The action taken against Ouranos is the first indication in the theogony that the natural cycles of the cosmos are not solely responsible for its phenomena. In this way the first *generational* distinction is created. By the same token, the Titans thus also constitute the first delimited set that cannot be augmented indefinitely.

When Kronos becomes sovereign among the Gods, he will swallow his children, hiding them in his *own* body, whereas Ouranos hides them in Gaia's. Kronos' children are counted by him as part of himself, while Ouranos' children are counted as part of their mother. The action of Ouranos is instinctual; his continuous intercourse with Gaia simply provides no opportunity for the children to count as something other than her. Kronos, by contrast, appropriates his children to himself, and is forced to relinquish them by being tricked into swallowing a stone. Kronos is subtle of mind, *ankylomêtês*, literally, with an intelligence that winds or turns back upon itself, and just so he turns his children's difference back into himself, until encountering the stone, which as inert matter and brute facticity embodies the limits of the realm which Kronos' son Zeus will rule, since the stone stands in for Zeus on the plane of Kronian intelligence, a boundary stone of irreducible difference. It is not that Kronian intelligence proves faulty with respect to the stone, but that the stone is unknowable on the former's terms.

To return, however, to the emergence of Aphrodite, we learn that the severed genitals of Ouranos fall into the sea, Pontus. Pontus belongs to the same 'generation' as Ouranos, and is likewise born from Gaia. But whereas Gaia produces Ouranos to be her equal, Pontus is generated "without *philotês*" (132) — friendship, love, affection. That is, he is generated in accord with the old order of Eros. Pontus goes on to generate his own child, Nereus (father of the Nereids), by the same parthenogenesis. The lines of Gaia's descendents through Pontus and through Ouranos do not unite at any point in Hesiod's account until Poseidon's intercourse with Medusa results in the conception of Pegasus the winged horse and Chrysaor the winged pig, which makes this latter event one of signal importance in Hellenic theology. Note, in this respect, that Pegasus and Chrysaor do not come to birth in normal fashion, either, but fly out of Medusa's neck after the hero Perseus has decapitated her. This represents another generational separation, in which a Goddess who is, paradoxically, *stipulated* to be mortal (Medusa), is decapitated, where we might compare the separation of head from body with the separation of genitalia from body in the case of Ouranos,[5] but this time by a hero, a child of a God and a mortal. The products of this operation belong thus to the 'heroic age', the procession of the potencies of the Gods into the mortal domain. Pegasus assists Bellerophon in his labors and then joins the Gods on Olympus as the carrier of Zeus' thunderbolts, method of communication between Olympus and the mundane world, while the head of Medusa becomes part of the weaponry of Athena, patroness of heroic labors and of cities.

---

[5] Or the separation of the spike or head of the wheat plant from the stem, the name 'Chrysaor' (golden blade) sometimes being identified with this.

I indulge in this digression in order to clarify, by looking at the union of the lines of Pontus and Ouranos in the subsequent generation, the foreshadowed union to be embodied in Aphrodite. Because the severed genitals of Ouranos fall *epi pontô*, into the sea, Aphrodite has in a sense two fathers and no mother. Pontus must be distinguished clearly from Okeanos, our sense of the word 'ocean' tending to confuse them. Okeanos is the source of all fresh water as well as of the ambrosia on which the Gods feast. His children are the rivers and the Okeanid nymphs, who belong, not to the ocean in our sense, but to the springs and other bodies of fresh water. Pontus, by contrast, is the salt sea, the 'fruitless deep'. It is possible that Aphrodite's emergence from the sea refers in some way to the sea's salt, its hidden potency, but it refers also to its fruitlessness, inasmuch as Aphrodite's concern will be less with the products of erotic activity than with this activity as a *medium*, just as the sea is a medium for the creatures who do not drink of it, as such, but incorporate it all throughout their tissues. The sea, too, is a medium for the traffic of vessels upon it, as mortal bodies, a kind of vessel, launch themselves through erotic attraction and activity onto the sea of embodied mortal life.

Pontus' other child, more conventionally conceived albeit with his mother Gaia, is Nereus, whose daughters are the Nereids, the sea-nymphs, most famous among whom is arguably Thetis, mother of Achilles. Thetis lends theological importance to the whole of the Trojan War, because she represents another generational break in the progress of cosmogenesis. The prophecy that she will bear a son greater than his father effectively forces a decision upon the Gods: either allow a further generation of Gods to whom the sovereignty will pass, so that what we know as the terminal organization of the divine realm would instead become medial, or force Thetis to marry a mortal. Peleus is the mortal, and he makes her his wife once he is able to prove himself master over her power of transformation. His name hints at this, as it seems to be related to the world *pêlos*, meaning clay. He will be able, thus, to receive and fix her fluctuating shape. This is a threshold that not Peleus alone, but all mortals as such must cross if these divine powers are to devolve upon them. Menelaus must perform the same task as Peleus in order to learn from Proteus how to return home when he is becalmed off the coast of Egypt. Mastery over the flux inherent in psychical being makes possible a further stage of cosmogenesis, marking the last generation of the 'heroic age'. Already in the image of Aphrodite emerging from the sea is a suggestion of a binding force hidden in the fluctuating element. In Plato's *Cratylus* (420a), Socrates speculates that "*erôs* is so called because it flows in [*esrei*] from without," to which we may compare Aphrodite "wafted … over the waves of the loud-moaning sea" in Homeric Hymn VI. Ares, too, shares in this wave-like action, being compared in the *Iliad*

(5.597-9) to "a swift-streaming river that floweth on to the sea ... seething with foam [*aphros*]," (trans. Murray). Aphrodite is associated with heroes both because they are products of the *erôs* between Gods and mortals, as Socrates puns in Plato's *Cratylus* (398c-d), but also, as we see in the myths of Ariadne and Theseus or of Medea and Jason, through the erotic bonds that draw the hero and heroine onward and supply the element crucial to the accomplishment of their quest.

The Trojan War is the site of the intensely conflictual emergence of this new moment in the formation of the cosmos. Platonists traditionally saw in the conflict a symbol for two levels of the soul. One, represented by the Trojans, is tied to the mortal body. Hence the Trojans defend their citadel whose walls were constructed by Poseidon (the demiurge of motion and thus of soul, according to Proclus)[6] in unpaid labor, this lack of remuneration suggesting the terminal nature of embodiment, while the Achaeans represent the other part of the soul, that which transmigrates. These two sides of the soul fight for possession of *embodied beauty*, Helen, who has been delivered into the mortal citadel through Aphrodite's activity, specifically because of Paris' choice. Paris chooses that the

---

[6] On Poseidon, see "Sea of Dissimilitude: Poseidon and Platonism," pp. 213-235 in *From the Roaring Deep: A Devotional in Honor of Poseidon and the Spirits of the Sea*, ed. Rebecca Buchanan (Asheville, NC: Bibliotheca Alexandrina, 2015).

golden apple, the symbol of sovereignty over the physical world, should be awarded to Aphrodite, rather than to Athena or Hera. Aphrodite is therefore, from this point of view, a cosmic demiurge, an artisan of the world's order, when Paris chooses his world, and so Empedocles does nothing truly radical by treating her as the condition of the possibility of his own cosmological discourse.[7]

Any of the choices Paris could have made would have had a sufficient rationale. Athena embodies the idealistic principle in civilization, and is the tip of the spear of the Olympian project. Hera, as wife and co-sovereign with Zeus, has a unique legitimacy in reigning over the world as constituted in time.[8] But Aphrodite is the eldest, and transcends the Olympian project narrowly conceived. This will be embodied in a very special way as a result of Paris' choice, on a plane at once theological, but which also embraces certain historical facts and the dynamic evolution of the very notion of what is the World. Aeneas, Aphrodite's son by the mortal Anchises, a rare instance in Hellenic theology of a

---

[7] M. R. Wright, *Empedocles: The Extant Fragments* (Indianapolis, IN: Hackett, 1995), frags. 8 (17 DK); 25 (22 DK); 60 (71 DK); 85-87 (86, 87, 95 DK).

[8] On Hera, see "Queen of *Kinêsis*: Understanding Hera," pp. 126-148 in *Queen of Olympos: A Devotional Anthology for Hera and Iuno*, ed. Lykeia (Asheville, NC: Bibliotheca Alexandrina, 2013).

child conceived in this fashion — Achilles, of course, is another — in founding Rome, inaugurates, in effect, a second heroic age which escapes the bounds of Hellenic theology as such. To extend the Platonic interpretation, the ruins of Troy are the shambles of mortality bereft of the intelligible, which has been spirited away whence it came. It presents an image in this way of sheer historical contingency. From this, however, and embodied in Aeneas, arises a new level of organization, the truly multi-ethnic empire, which must have Aphrodite as its patron because it supersedes the political organization of the *ethnos*. The international imperial organization, and the new 'cosmopolitan' concept of citizenship it implies, is grounded therefore in the Ouranian, Titanic Aphrodite.

The Hellenistic and Imperial age thus constitutes an Aphrodisian epoch of sorts. It is an age of new myths, and whenever new heroes emerge, Aphrodite is necessarily involved. As discussed by Michel Foucault in *The Care of the Self*, a new rhetoric of conjugality emerges in this period, as well as the literary form of the romance novel. Furthermore, the role of the hero as child of humans and Gods becomes significantly augmented in the images of the Christ as well as the deified Roman emperors. These phenomena point, perhaps, to the attempt at symbolically appropriating that aspect of Aphrodite signified by the epithet *pandêmos*. When the Empire, for whatever pragmatic reasons, granted citizenship to all free men and women living within its borders in 212 CE under Caracalla, it formalized something born in fact much earlier, namely the institution of citizenship in a sense not tied to ethnicity. Purely formal though it may have been, it represents a milestone in a project of symbolic appropriation that continues into the present day.

Homer, in contrast to Hesiod, presents Zeus and the titaness Dione as Aphrodite's parents (*Iliad* 5.370 & sqq.). Doubtless this is true for the realm treated in Homer's poem, the cosmic plane answering to Paris' choice. The Aphrodite of this realm fathers a mortal son, and she is even wounded in the psychical strife constitutive of this plane. Aphrodite thus, like Eros, is in a sense born again within the Olympian organization. The name of Dione is so closely linked with that of Zeus etymologically as to suggest the feminine complements common in Egyptian theology. Hence in Egypt Amun has his feminine hypostasis, Amaunet, who, however her status be understood, is in any case clearly as distinct from Amun's divine partner Mut as is Dione from Zeus' partner Hera. If Dione be understood as in some analogous sense as a feminine hypostasis of Zeus himself, then Aphrodite's emergence from Zeus and Dione would bear a certain functional kinship with the birth of Athena from Zeus and Metis, daughter of Okeanos and Tethys and first wife of Zeus according to Hesiod (886-7) whose *mêtis* (wisdom, skill, craft)

Zeus has appropriated to himself.[9] Indeed, Athena is born from the *mêdea* (counsels or plans) of Zeus as Aphrodite is born from the *mêdea* (genitals) of Ouranos.

This kinship between Aphrodite and Athena relative to Zeus would underscore a 'political' function for Aphrodite, one which differs, however, from Athena's in pertaining to the cosmo-polis, but which similarly expresses Zeus' sovereignty.[10] This sovereignty of Zeus', of course, comes at the price of his vulnerability to the power exercised by his 'daughter', in which the irreducible presence of Aphrodite as daughter of primordial Ouranos shines through the Homeric fabric. It should be noted that Aphrodite can receive the epithet *Ourania* even when she is said to be the daughter of Zeus, as in a

---

[9] The Okeanid Metis also resembles the Nereid Thetis in certain respects: both are the subject of a prophecy concerning their potential offspring, and according to pseudo-Apollodorus (*Bibliotheca* 1.20), Metis takes on a series of different forms when Zeus tries to couple with her, as Thetis does with Peleus.

[10] Aphrodite is identified with *eros* in the political sphere in the form of Aphrodite Pandêmos, Aphrodite of the body public, the *res publica*, the commons. This aspect of Aphrodite is sometimes regarded, rather cynically, as referring to her as patron either of prostitution or at any rate of 'merely' carnal love; but in fact in this form Aphrodite secures the bonds which make any politics possible, the basic sense of community. In addition, through her epithet *Hêgemonê*, Aphrodite is worshiped in military contexts as securing the bond between commanders and subordinates (Pironti, chap. 4 §64).

fragment of Euripides' lost drama *Phaethon* (F 781, 228-30). In Orphic fragments reported by Proclus (*In Crat*. 110.18-111.5), Aphrodite's two births both come from seed falling into the sea, the first in a manner essentially identical to Hesiod's account, while in the second Zeus simply releases his seed into the sea. Proclus says that Dione "assists" Zeus in this, without further specification. If she does so by hand, this would invite comparison with the role of Iusâas in the Egyptian Heliopolitan cosmogony.

A further difference in how Aphrodite presents herself for Hesiod and for Homer is in her marital ties. For Hesiod, she is paired with Ares, to whom she bears Phobos and Deimos, and daughter Harmonia, who marries Kadmos and becomes grandmother to the Theban hypostasis of Dionysos. The pairing of Aphrodite and Ares is by far the common one outside of Homer's *Odyssey*.[11] In the *Odyssey*, by contrast, Aphrodite's lawful union is with Hephaistos, her union with Ares illicit. No tradition, however, even those which present Aphrodite and Hephaistos as a pair (for example, Apollonius Rhodius' *Argonautica*) speaks of a child of their union, unless we identify Aphrodite and Aglaia, with whom Hephaistos is paired in the *Iliad* (18.382), Aglaia being one of the Charites, who are associated with Aphrodite. Hesiod, too, for his part, makes Aglaia the wife of Hephaistos (*Theogony*

---

[11] Pironti, chap. 4, §52 & sqq. gathers evidence for the ubiquity of the association between Aphrodite and Ares.

945). If we allow Aphrodite to absorb Aglaia, then her four children by Hephaistos according to an Orphic fragment are Eukleia, Euthenia, Eupheme, and Philophrosyne, who form the group of 'younger Charites', embodying seemingly a set of more narrowly defined social virtues than the more well-known trinity of Charites. The traditions with respect to the Charites and their relationships to deities of whom they are the offspring or consorts or companions in whatever respect are too diverse and, from a theological viewpoint, too lightly cast to allow one to say more than that clearly the entire world of the Charites belongs on the side of the union between Aphrodite and Hephaistos, rather than on that of Aphrodite and Ares.

The products of the union of Aphrodite and Ares, by contrast, are literally 'fear' and 'dread', demonstrating that these latter phenomena are not alien to Aphrodite's nature. Aphrodite's bonds lead to souls' mortal embodiment,[12] and then to their attachments to one another in this state, which are the preconditions for fear and dread. The primordial nature of this connection, moreover, allows us to see the common ground between the traditional account and that of the *Odyssey* inasmuch as the *Odyssey* frames Aphrodite's and Ares' relationship as a bond outside the law, but by that very fact, as a

---

[12] Plutarch, *Amatorius* 20, speaks of souls awaiting return to mortal embodiment in "the meadows of Selene and Aphrodite."

spontaneous attraction, *prior to law*, belonging to the domain of what could not be legislated in any case, just as the mortal attachments to one's own person and to those one loves place limits on the law's application in numerous contexts.

Gabrielle Pironti's book *Entre ciel et guerre* could be considered in its entirety an argument for the essential harmony of Aphrodite and Ares, not as complementary opposites, as 'love' and 'war' in a simplistic sense, but as divinities concerned with the very same sphere of activity, namely that in which mortals stake their very being. In a particularly striking parallel, both Aphrodite and Ares are wounded in the Trojan War.[13] As Pironti puts it, "The vulnerability of Ares, just like that of Aphrodite, is inseparable from his domain of action. The God who presides over war's bodily intimacy is naturally found, on the narrative plane, to be affected by all the dangers and sorrows which menace the combatants: wounds, pain, and depletion of the vital force ... Bodies exposed, on the line, Ares and Aphrodite resemble one another indeed."[14]

---

[13] Aphrodite at *Iliad* 5.335 & sqq., Ares at 5.855 & sqq.

[14] Pironti, chap. 4, §19, translation mine.

Aphrodite: Mystique and Mysterium: The Breath of the Soul Is the Heart of the Matter

by Iona Miller

Your heart knows in silence the secrets of the days and the nights. But your ears thirst for the sound of your heart's knowledge. — Gibran

The union of man and woman is like the mating of Heaven and Earth. It is because of their correct mating that Heaven and Earth lust forever. Humans have lost this secret and have therefore become mortal. By knowing it the Path to Immortality is opened. — Shang-Ku-San-Tai.

It is not easy to make an honest attempt to find words for the ineffable. Like unashamed Aphrodite, this essay hopes to titillate, to provoke, to promise even more than it may deliver. The naked mysteries and hidden charms of existence are concealed and revealed. We will flirt with ideas, but won't cover all of her aspects, exploits, or relationships. We may even mix metaphors, or skip promiscuously from subject to subject like a restless dreamer.

We all have a keen grasp of the obvious when it comes to love goddess myths and basic psychology. Culture is part of our nature. Hopefully, each reader — anyone who has had or lost a love, or is a devotee of the goddess — will find their own revelations arising within from the unconscious. A psychological approach to Aphrodite as image-making capacity attends and tends passionately to both psyche and logos.

Image and words are the interplay of sensation, intuition, thinking, and feeling. Born into Chronos, our two million year old soul longs for Kairos, Spirit's time is the opportune or crucial moment for significant change. Every moment is an opportunity if we tend and attend to it.

Aphrodite, the divine Beloved, is the unseen third being that informs every relationship and devotion. We suggest an archetypal sense of her in the world at large, beyond our libidinous cravings. Tending the heart is minding the soul. Imaginal figures invite us to share the wisdom of our own inner landscapes, dreams, intuitive callings, visions, feelings, and events. All the functions of the psyche converge in fantasy, in imagination. We are all equally prone to the seductions of our own inner images, thoughts, emotions, and sensations.

Ritual action brings a larger view of self and world. But technique is not soul. Aphrodite's mystique is her sacred presence in the ordinary, inherent beauty apprehended as soul. But the creative power of language and the poetic is also a natural feature of reality. Imagination and language transform the soul through Mystery.

Aphrodite is born of the primal serpent of the energy ocean that spans time and space. A cosmic principle, Love is the ultimate symbol of a continuous process of participatory transformation, which can be glorious, painful, irreversible, and essential. Energies associated with the deity change our outlook, perceptions and feelings through communion with the intimate otherness of the world. The world becomes a more enlivened place.

We experience our own imaginal essence through the power of love and other structures of human experience, the *archai*. The power of Aphrodite is an expression of the divine whose trans-sensory organ of perception is imagination. Raw nature, fertile chaos, lies at the heart of the psyche — the wild energies of creation. Love is a path for consciously realized life. Imaginal love plays a central role in human life that softens the heart.

Whether activated or dormant, the vital principle still living in our substance and essence, re-enchants the world. There is more to life than just matter. The unconscious modifies the conscious. The invisible force of animation is an immense force of nature — metaphysical, biological, and phenomenological resonance.

We call such awesome emotional intensity a numinous experience. We are aroused by the power, presence, or realization of a divinity — an uncanny, mighty spirit, a tremendous mystery. True imagination embodies the divine wisdom of the soul through percepts, affect, and concepts. Aphrodite is our image making capacity.

Only when the soul enters the material cosmos is there need to honor its generative power, to make a relationship with the divine through that particular worldview. Aphrodite is a living system, the cycle of life and love, complexes of experiences in which we participate, where duality is expressed as the sublimated quest of alliance.

The light in nature is the divine in the world. Myth, the interplay of cosmic principles, and memory are the basis of our relationships. The root of existence is matter and spirit, including that of Aphrodite — the deep nature of reality and experience, veiling and revealing its divinity.

The image freely gives itself, inviting sustained attention. We can watch our soul when we embrace the image. When the emerging god-image remains unconscious and unintegrated, it expresses as archetypal opposites instead of unpolarized consciousness.

All archetypes bring more than one archetypal pattern with them — positive and negative, concealed and revealed, healthy and destructive. Fantasy precedes the symbol which flowers spontaneously in the soul and is more potent and descriptive than fantasy. Such fields of potential have forceful intentionality and complete autonomy. We are all aware of the slings and arrows love exerts beyond the sentimental moments through all the seasons of the heart.

Rather than us coming to the gods, it is more they who come to us. We are called by her when the soul is called by love of the phenomenal image. This is also an integrative, deep imagery-based approach to therapy. Our deepest impulses of the soul take on a divine shape, mythical configurations. We see by means of dynamic patterns, forms and textures.

The invisible — the unseen aspect of our existence — is revealed through visible images and shapes. We just need sensitivity to the image to contact the hidden depths of the soul. We don't need to theorize, interpret, or understand the uncanny and irrational for them to work on us, independent of our thinking. Psychic development leads toward self-understanding. The mystery is not knowledge but experience.

To worship her is a world affirming theurgy that invokes the world soul. By working on and through us, the goddess manifests as the living spirit of creation and divine consciousness in matter. Only by living soul's embodied experience, embodied agonies, and experiential knowing can we determine if the suffering is worth the trajectory.

Our breath is our mantra. The primary relationship of our soul is with the soul of the world, the divine spark in every cell of creation. By bridging the opposites, soul weaves cosmos into existence. The mystery of turning lead into gold is a revelation of the hidden light within the darkness of matter.

Primordial Images

Aphrodite is the basis of formative aspects of the unconscious, the spiritual seed of creation, the relativity of psychological processes, peak experiences, and libidinal transference. She is the radiant emptiness beyond our self-image and worldview, beyond our sense and sensory projections. Soul illuminates the body.

In the cleavage between creation and redemption is the breath of the *anima mundi*, the macrocosmic world-pervading element of space itself. Remembering to breathe grounds us from the spinning mind, in which we can lose ourselves. She unites the whole mindbody with universe. The numinous appears as the sacredness of creative acts.

As all archetypes, she is aggressive, possessive, and very jealous. All compulsions are pressures of the archetype, but we don't like to dis-identify from it, even when it is harming our humanness. Such force overwhelms the ego, possesses the ego from unconscious wish to manifest behavior. We are subjected to fragmentation and reshaping. In her liminal space we abandon our previous identities.

But we need to honor it, without identifying with it or being inflated by its numinosity. The strongest religious experience happens in crisis. Without containment the numinous annihilates the ego and structural field with unconscious associative attachments.

Aphrodite's siren call is seductive,

enormously tempting and powerful. She fills us with energy, vision, and a sense of meaning. Feeling wonderful, it is hard to simply feel ordinary again. If you don't honor it, because of primitive grandiosity you think you are it — a god[dess]. This thing is unconscious within us, and we try to find somebody to embody and hold that significant energy for us.

Thinking you are it, you act it out. It is destructive for yourself and others. She is a natural phenomenon, therefore amoral, so we are charged with the issue of ethics in relation to her, because a potent or creative person is either a dangerous person or potentially great. Jung suggests that when you "do with conviction the next and most necessary thing, you are always doing something meaningful and intended by fate."

Aphrodite's name is one of many we give to the voice and vision of the unconscious which can reunite us through transformation with the unconscious source of our creativity and our divine source, however we conceive it — the variety of forms through which we realize the self.

Relating to an image is like relating to an entity. If we create a space, unconscious content manifests as personifications open to dialogue and exploration. They come when they want to come but are explicitly anchored in our lives in some way.

Vision is perceived by intense concentration on the background of consciousness. We try to grasp its significance to us, apart from the tyranny of the literal. We seek the affirming glow of a love story. We concoct our narrative, but is it fiction, romance, or wisdom literature? It includes the irrationals: synchronicity, beauty, truth, grief, and love.

Until then, we practice the Art of longing. We have a longing for belonging. We are cut off from our ancestral voices and relationships in the technological society. Thus, we don't know who we are and where we come from, much less where we are going. The cliche is "the heart wants what it wants." Some things are best seen through the eyes of those we love.

Typically, in a midlife crisis we go looking for a special or magical person, a fantasy of the transformation process. In our Dark Night, we experience fear, anxiety and in some cases panic, as we lose sight of our purpose, our goals and a bright future. We may feel abandoned, helpless and depressed; our self-compassion suffers. We naturally seek the known or unknown person that embodies rebirth for us, yearning for their love.

Aphrodite is about relationships, being related, not just to a family or partner, but to the depths, to the calling that wounds and names us, to the Soul of the World. Soul is in and of the world in both the open and attentive broken heart which allows the gods to penetrate through our wounds. Truth grows organically from deep roots in the body, through investigating the secret language of nature and our own nature. Love or the lack of it is the context in which we live our lives.

We break up, we break down, and sometimes break out. Soul is heard through the symptom if we listen carefully, acknowledge, and recognize it, in our blind instinct, fascinations, projections, and participation mystique with the herd. To be conscious in the present is to be solitary.

Social containers keep us undifferentiated, unable to break up into individual personalities. Jung cautions that participation mystique with the herd is submersion in a common unconsciousness. "Every step forward means tearing oneself loose from the maternal womb of unconsciousness in which the mass of men dwells."

Existentially, Aphrodite has always been with us unconsciously, in our ongoing fantasies, native connectivity and kindness. We sometimes notice her myth playing through our life giving it 'reality.' But rapture and ecstasy are passive states that happen to us, that come over us.

Rainer Maria Rilke suggested, "Let everything happen to you — beauty and terror. Just keep going, no feeling is final." Intensity moves us from need to want to desire to consuming passion. We can get lost in our relationships, in our psychic gaps, with groups and individuals. Identified with the group in participation mystique, a relic of the primordial unconscious state of mystical connection, we cannot distinguish ourselves from it. We feel whole because we 'belong,' but we aren't.

The powers of life and death always speak

mythologically, connecting the ideal and the ordinary. Love fertilizes the psyche. They help us to not 'lose heart' in a rapidly-changing overwhelming world. As the Delphic Oracle said, "Called or uncalled, the god is present." Our task is to grasp this psychic process, and embrace it with our thinking, feeling, sensation, and intuition as our paths of orientation. Thinking and sensation are complimented by the intuition and feeling of our spiritual nature.

Life & Death

We are born naked and go down to the grave stripped of personality with a bare soul or psyche. Aphrodite was goddess of love to both the living and departed souls. In her more archaic form as Hathor, she also had a heavenly and underworld form, and made a descent to the underworld like Inanna. The primeval goddess helped women give birth. She welcomed the dead to the next life and helped the dead to be reborn. Hathor renews the cosmos, even the unseen depths of the unconscious.

From the field of mythological expressions, Aphrodite mobilizes and mediates universal motifs or repetitive images and nature's creative response. Our image of the world is our worldview, or mental model of reality — a philosophy or conception of the world. Such presuppositions condition our outlook and ground how we perceive life in the cosmos.

Deeper understanding of existence is the

heart our knowledge. Worldview exerts a crucial influence on our thinking and behavior. This set of beliefs about Reality grounds our way of perceiving, thinking, knowing, and doing. It is the basis of our cosmology, metaphysics, teleology, epistemology, theology, and anthropology — even our love life.

Through a union of our physical and psychological aspects, psyche mirrors both with anthropomorphic qualities. We project a body on the goddess, a haunting otherness, that corresponds with our own constitution. We perceive it with the senses and a self-conscious psyche, reflecting the god we imagine.

Our grasp of the psyche, vital psychic phenomena, and the unknown darkness that surrounds us is limited. But we know god-images exist, in general and in particular. In much the same way, we may never know who our human partners really are, but we have a relationship, including all sorts of unknown factors and projections. We have experiences with imagination, substance, and body.

Myth reveals our divine life. The gods still reign within. Living figures confront us autonomously. Libido is the creative power of our own soul, bringing forth the useful and the harmful. Love's opposite is the power shadow — power vs. love, or pleasure in hurting.

A psychological fact, Aphrodite grips us when we 'fall into temptation,' or love falls on us from above, determining our destiny (*amor fati*).

The shadow of Aphrodite appears as conquest-oriented seduction, love and sex addiction, an inability to say no to passion, or being totally destroyed when a lover leaves.

Love is ambiguous: it can be terrible, even self-destructive or self-realizing.

Rather than speak of being in love, the ancients claimed they were hit or possessed by a god. The archaic love relationship is a Marriage with God. Sex becomes love of the divine (*amor Dei*). The transpersonal is symbolized by the King and Queen, god and goddess.

The unconscious merges with the physiological body, including joy, stress, pain, and symptoms. Even love penetrates us as an ailment — we are "lovesick" with or without it. We sometimes fear it is beyond our human capacity to endure. We yearn for the very source of yearning. If we yearn for, or even if we imagine we have 'lost' Aphrodite, certain conditions can bring her back in full force.

Subtle Bodies

Our subtle body is personal anima, which echoes the transpersonal Anima Mundi, or Aphrodite, the breath soul that causes and bridges the gap between mind and physical body. She is everything that breathes or is breathed. She is our philosophical potential. The body of the world and its psyche reflect the goddess we imagine. Jung quotes an alchemical text that says, "The mind should learn compassionate love for the body." (Jung-Ostrowski, p. 25)

What we call spirit is the living body seen from within, and body is its outer manifestation. Spirit and body are really functional psychic modalities. Body as psyche is an expression of interiority. We give body to our thoughts by speaking or expressive arts, so we can share them by making them perceptual in the ordinary world.

Only the living body contains the intelligent secret of life, but the anatomical body doesn't really inform us about the nature of matter. The body has its own psychological condition and consciousness.

We thrive by maintaining a conscious relationship to the body, where the rights of the body and spirit are equivalent. Archetypes and bodily functions follow universal instinctive patterns. They can be reduced in shame to "mere" instincts, or overvalued as gods in a grandiose or addictive way, rather than at human scale — a human representation.

The opposites are united in the soul through primordial experience of the outer world and inherent divinity. Though we don't know how, we experience them as numinous events. Aphrodite is a biological, instinctual, and elemental "model," mediating between human consciousness and the primordial numinous experience. But sometimes we are fooled by our own interpretations, instead of simply being aware of immediate experience. We have to follow a rather uncertain path.

We encounter her spellbinding personal

aspects and transformative collective aspects that move us from one state of consciousness to another, and another. Myths and their cosmic dramas shape and reshape us and the beliefs that influence our behavior. The ordinary body is transformed into the eternally enduring body, at least symbolically or metaphorically.

The earthly Aphrodite of 'ordinary' love is suspended between our ascents to her cosmic nature and chthonic (material) descents. Our animal soul leads us down into the depths of our body, our instinct symbolized as Aphrodite's familiars, which include the serpent, a symbol of kundalini.

Her highest truths spring from the roots of the body, or our psychic experience of the body as shown in dreams. But we tear this experience of body and spirit apart with the mind, separating them with concepts. We only know a small part of our psyche like we have limited awareness of our internal physiology.

We have centers of consciousness in our head, heart, and abdomen which we experience as our psychic image of the body. Body, soul, and mind are one, but we parse them into categories.

Their reunification is rebirth, the hermaphrodite, the stone, the golden flower. So, the 'reborn body' is spirit at the same time — the glorified body that unites spiritual and material principles. An eternal or subtle body at least symbolically ensures the continuity of our detached consciousness, but represents our future potential —

our unknown and as-yet-unrealized potential.

Mind is related to body (matter) as body is to earth. We must return to our body for true individuation. The psychophysical self embodies our past as memory. The body is our subconscious memory and mirror of our experience. The indestructible body is the integrated personality, the refined psyche filled with inherent light.

Notions of gods are the first of all myths, vital psychic phenomena symbolizing the powers of the unconscious. We may not know what a god or archetype 'is,' but we can 'know' them and interact with that image spiritually, and experience it psychologically, and metaphorically. It may be essentially unknowable, but is intense and compelling. For some, primordial experience of the source means the sanctuary and refuge of the deity, only present in direct experience.

Our experience of love and loss changes our beliefs about it and the pain we can experience from attachments, as well as lessons we learn from it. Some open us to reconciliation and renewal. Our particular life solutions lie only along our particular life path or trajectory. Without general solutions, problems are answered only through our individuality.

The instinctive drive overtakes and consumes our personality. Sexual passion has been deified, divinized, or even feared as evil and demonic because of its overwhelming nature. In the real world sex often isn't associated with love, even when respectful or consensual. Many experiences can awaken us to a shock-receiving capacity.

We passion bearers find out who we are through our difficulties, life passages, and turning points. We break open to our impediments and destinies. The unconscious comes to life in all of its awful glory. An inner impulse motivates us, especially at critical times. Visions spring from the unconscious as spontaneous phenomena; so does a new sense of wonder.

Love is our main motive power and shapes our lives — in dream, or vision, or passionate encounter. Nature and beauty have a divine origin beyond common love. The unmediated vision is instantaneous experience. As for psychic life, we join mystery to mystery to create a portrait of a Mystery. We borrow and distort images from our actual experience that surge up from the mists of the past.

The mysteries of life are hidden between the opposites, including fullness and emptiness. Consciousness is born of suffering when we are shaken by naked truths that will not be comforted. In failure we find that there are driving forces. We're here for deeper life experience that funds our compassion, rapport, and empathy with weight and importance.

Affect, another word for god, forms and shapes us with unconscious determinants. The divine impresses our inner experience. High-level networks of control make decisions long before they enter awareness. Our body and behavioral patterns carry our stories, our symbolic life of depth and meaning. Images reveal complex relationships, tensions, and interconnections. Something huge has shifted.

Ritual, fusing desire and action for effective change, helps us connect with and transform inner polarities. Living with depth from the unconscious beings brings a pervasive sense of the sacred. The task of generativity after midlife is opening liminal space for personal and collective evolution and cosmic consciousness. Whatever soul touches becomes numinous. Gibran invites us to touch it with our fingers as "the naked body of your dreams."

The mythic world we forget in daylight comes to us in dreams. No one can faithfully paint a dream, because felt-sense is perhaps the biggest part of it. The inner experience gives rise unconsciously to its expression. Beauty and soul run into fable and personification, the metaphorical and lyrical perspective.

Psychic elements rearrange themselves into images which have effects. They are immanent in natural law and active in phenomena associated with the supernatural and spiritual. Fantasy and imagination merge and interpenetrate. Ideas and facts merge in interpretation of events, images, and networks of learning. We integrate and embody Aphrodite, affirming her presence as the sacred psyche.

Archetypal Nature

Love reveals our essential nature as the presence of the sacred. Phenomena are revealed in patterns. When she transports us, desire becomes self-revelation, a supernatural dynamic that multiplies the forces of life, mirrored in the ancient love goddesses. We are chosen by something greater than ourselves. We now understand gods are archaic psychic processes within ourselves, autonomous psychic entities. Soul is the form-giving principle of the body and outer life.

Aphrodite is an archetypal field of eroticism. We wonder what hit us; we are flooded with emotion. The goddess captivates our imagination. She breaks us open to love and loss. The awe-inspiring force of desire and sex, the unconscious drive, has played a role in religion, magic, mysticism, occultism, and symbolism. She is the creative wellspring of art.

This is the breath of life. Aphrodite means the literal exchange of radiant life-force with the environment. When we breathe in unison we create rapport and impact. She 'wells up' from our depths as the water of life.

The fountain inside us wants to open up and pour out the living waters from the sacred ground of divine darkness. Immanence is an existential reality — immersion in the uncreated light — at least phenomenologically and psychologically, if not religiously. Creative spirit transmutes darkness to light. But the body is the present moment — here and now, aesthetically alive to the world.

If we don't reduce it to psychological common sense but stick to the phenomenology, we see what animates from there. We still use mythological symbols and metaphors such as 'illumination.' Affects motivate us and form images. Psyche reflects timeless and spaceless perceptions, reverberations beyond the immediate. Our whole psychobiology interacts with the transpersonal — the timeless world of the seemingly eternal.

Primordial human desires are not mainly concerned with possibility, but with desirability, and energy beyond striving. We discover what we have to give the world and what the world has to give to us beyond seduction and 'bedroom eyes.' Beauty matters, but is proverbially more than skin deep. Thus, we refine our character.

Like truth and goodness, beauty helps us see the world of here and now with more meaning. Beauty dawns on us, shines on us from ordinary things, and connects us with the sacred. The real appears transfigured in the light of the ideal. Timeless moments, such as dappled sunlight, an awesome vista, recalling the face of a loved one, suddenly make life worth living.

We imagine the heart as the basis of emotional life. We grasp the world not only through the senses, but through the unconscious psychic substrate. The divine is a dynamic bond inside waiting to be found and redeem us.

In our deepest core feelings we are most vulnerable to pain, momentary unbalance, and divine frenzy. When the unconscious is activated through love it coincides in an uncanny way with objective events. Coincidence with meaning is always there, but it lights up.

Soul Guide

Aphrodite is a soul-guide and her myth is therapeutic. The eternal mother and source of all creation is the generative spirit — root and ground of every soul and fountain of heaven and earth. She is with us on the threshold of life's greatest decisions.

Aphrodite is the living psyche which means soul, in the psychological, but not religious sense. Soul is existential unity of the self. It has no extension but it has interiority where we face the deep core of emptiness. It is therefore not simply about 'getting horizontal,' but the verticality of connecting to the heights and depths of knowledge and passion. Our inner nature and greater Nature is a psychic reflection of the whole world.

Soul has a certain awareness, a non-ordinary perceptual framework, that includes our nonphysical aspects. Consciousness, wisdom, mind, thought, clairvoyance, feeling, intuition, and will seem distinct from the physical body. But real ideas and imagination have blood in them. Soul is our feelings — our embodied emotional and moral nature, our hidden most private thoughts and feelings, even embedded memories — our worldview.

It isn't what you look at, but what you see with the Art of Seeing. We are rewarded with the blessing of transparency and deepened insight into the world and the soul. Goethe said, "Everyone sees what he carries in his heart." William Blake said, "Without unceasing Practice nothing can be done: Practice is Art. If you leave off you are lost." (Appendix to *The Prophetic Books*)

Conceptual analysis of romantic love can be rather dry, with cliche or predictable tropes. Hollywood institutionalized it. This deity of love and sexual lust can be from a ruling pantheon or a mortal considered a 'goddess of love.' Male love gods are included in this trope. It is called "Love Goddess" rather than "Love Deity" because females are much more common. They merge and emerge in the symbolic divine hermaphrodite.

Aphrodite's Mystique

Call her what you will — Venus, Aphrodite, Cybele, Inanna, Ishtar, Asherah, Shekinah, Astarte, Cybele, Hathor, Bhavani, Shakti, Freya, Erzuli, Ochun (Black Aphrodite), or any other goddesses of love's mysteries. Her nature and stories are so paradoxical, it is a challenge to believe them all at once, but such is the domain of faith.

Aphrodite easily captures our devotion with her allure and delightful boons. Devotion to the divine, in whatever form or non-form we care to imagine, is the unveiling of soul. She is the light of the soul — unsuppressed being. In her, soul and body are one.

Love transports our souls into the mythic dimension where it renews or destroys depending on our fate. The sensational realm of the Love Goddess is the immediate experience that veils our subconscious relationship to our own unconscious sexuality and power motives.

We all worship Aphrodite informally. We devote ourselves to her arts in an effort to attract and thrive with the love we all naturally need. She is the goddess of mutual desire and emotional experience with others (friendship, understanding, soul connection, rapport, empathy), and consummation of relationships.

Aphrodite conveys a sense of immortality through the oceanic bliss of love and the sensation of timelessness when we are swept away in the thundering surf of desire and orgasm. When spirit as source energy and matter as form are in balance, the body becomes the living "Temple of the Spirit." A sense of immortality deepens the sacred dimension of life. Soul's immortality is sensed in direct experience of non-spatial, non-temporal, nonlocal, non-ordinary reality.

By honoring the sensual self, the metaphysical nature of surrender to the erotic impulse is experientially revealed as a glimpse of non-dual reality. The non-dual Heart is radiating as all creation, and blessing all creation, and singing this while embracing eternity. God meets Goddess, Emptiness and Form, Wisdom and Compassion, Agape and Eros, Ascent and Descent — perfectly and blissfully united.

This is the Way of Devotion, with all of its illusions, projections, hopes, and dreams. The same feeling strikes lovers and spiritual devotees (Bhakti yoga). In intimate relations, both parties are utterly changed by such encounters.

The nature of Beauty is an immediate self-revelation of things as they are: unity, line, rhythm, tension, elegance. Aesthetic arrest stops us in our tracks in communion with the inner and outer mysteries of the soul.

We should not lose sight of the fact that a big part of our sexuality takes place in our dreams, from which we can draw inspiration and self-knowledge otherwise hidden. We don't have to act out all facets of our sexuality. Our dreams and imagination inform us as much as real life.

The felt-sense of form and beauty is instinctual. In the union of body, soul, and spirit, the lead of the psychosexual self is transmuted or transubstantiated into the gold of a life lived from the higher Self, self-actualization, or an intentional life.

The depth dimension of mutual attraction is a poetic and aesthetic act, a celebratory rite, and a marriage of matter and spirit in an experience of wholeness. Aesthetic response is an essential emotional aspect of alchemy.

Emptiness and fullness flow together in words and images. This flow state is lyrical, epic, and dramatic. Aesthetic signification is one thing, but the deep emotional impact of aesthetic arrest — being suspended for a thrilling moment in the eternal — stops us in our tracks in a radiant instant of self-realization or immortal beauty.

We don't need to support that phenomenon with any theory, jargon or interpretation. Sex is an inherently healing practice that promotes well-being. It embraces rapport, reverie, and rebirth, an unobservable psychic process beyond sense perception.

Breath of Life

Aphrodite is the hot, moist breath of the soul, the deep breath of life. Awareness rests in the sensations of breath, the rapture of being alive, transcending thought. In love, she is every breath we take (inhalation and exhalation and the gap between), every heartbeat, and the polarities of psyche. Whether in awe of Nature or in aesthetic arrest, we gasp in wonder that takes our breath away.

Aphrodite is air become rising breath — the very "breath of life." And words are made of nothing but breath — living psyche. The Word is the creative act, including the language of our instincts. Only that living breath connects us to the fact of all existence.

Mistress of the Labyrinth, Aphrodite-Ariadne (goddess of paths, wine, snakes, passion, and fertility) symbolizes vast convoluted mazes of entangled memories and trans-generational relationships. The monster at the center of the maze is a symbol of animal desire, carnal needs, and fleshly pursuits. The hero conquers and transcends it.

This serpentine path represents a soul journey to our own center and back again to the world with that sacred connection. On our individual path we overcome our own obstacles and expose our own illusions.

The Heart of the Matter

Aphrodite informs the heart of the journey. Our loyalty and devotion is the strength of the bond to Aphrodite — respect for what is sacred in our relationships with the gods, a feminine gnosis, and eroticism. Participatory wisdom suggests bringing the sacred back into the material realm. The aspirant balances the four psychic elements of instinctual awareness — earth, air, fire, and water.

In every meaningful way, the body is the subconscious mind, with the heart as its 'brain.' We honor the captivating Aphrodite when we imagine the world as our lover, with naked awareness, rapt attention, and self-revelation. Such contact with an enlivened sense of immediacy is a mind-body-spirit approach to personal transformation. We honor Aphrodite when we honor the World Soul.

We consciously worship her when we adore our beloved, making the conjugal bed an altar. In fact, it alters everything. The wisdom of the Tree of Knowledge is that sexuality isn't just in the gonads, but permeates every cell and atom of our bodies.

Aphrodite is an attitude or style of consciousness and behavior through which we fulfill legitimate psychophysical needs. She not only engenders but enlarges life with the mystical splendor of love. In some poetic sense, our very atoms and molecules, as well as the galaxies, are held together by the attractive force of love.

In the symbolic life, we re-experience the death-and-rebirth process, over and over again, just as we experience the 'petit mort' ("little death") of orgasm and renewal in our sexual lives. Imagination uses belief, thought, and visualization to impact the physical or biological root. We are hers when we devotedly pursue the inner images, thoughts, feelings, impulses, and urges.

Aphrodite's myth remains contemporary and aspirational — a psychosexual *satori*. The eternal nature of the divine reminds us that transcendence cannot be put on a timeline of temporal concreteness.

The unconscious nucleus of meaning of the eternal archetype remains "unborn" but her specific meaning and form, imagery and affects permeate us. If Aphrodite is eternal, eros is an event of specific temporality. Perhaps in a faithless world, the transitory and temporal hold the only redemptive power possible.

From Cybele to Symbol

There is a long list of obvious divine attributions backed by great literature as well as personal and collective experience. Aphrodite inspires a compelling, subjective state. Euripides called love the "breathes (or blasts) of Aphrodite." She seeks intimacy, touching the most private aspects of our lives. Aphrodite is linked with many lovers in different myths.

Aphrodite's symbol is the ankh-cross, symbol of the millions of years of life to come. The inexhaustible essence of the life force is a key of life that represents physical and immortal life and death, male and female balance, art, knowledge wisdom, reproduction, and sexual union. Her cosmology is that all life is connected with an interwoven animating energy, naked fullness, and loving receptivity.

Her sensuality is an irresistible blend of image, imagination, and happy or painful memory of the senses — the lapse of memory or precise memory of a smell, a touch, a look, a feeling. Under the spell of temptation we tend to 'forget who we are.' We say, even 'misery loves company.' In committed relationships, we conspire to build a single mutual body with mutual memories and mutual field of perception.

Beauty is transporting. Aphrodite is the mysterious, awe-inspiring something that comes over us when we are overcome. Lust incites intoxication, chaos, and destruction beyond that of love. To be, we must be perceived, mirrored back to ourselves by the immediate intimacy of others.

Psyche mirrors matter. What is Above mirrors that which is down Below. When we look out at Nature happening, it is us — no longer left outside, but embodied self-reflexivity — embodying the symbolic mirror of Aphrodite.

An ensouled world mirrors our own love, death, sorrow, happiness and much more. We see through the surface of a world that needs mirroring. We don't need to burden images with too many meaningful ideas as much as let them live and breath through us. Her meaning is form itself, here and now. Essence shines through appearance — the divinity of form in shape itself.

Soul reveals itself spontaneously and irrationally. It amplifies our understanding of observed phenomena. A flow of ideas arises from the image. We develop a dark-adapted eye for the unexpected or less apparent. A narrative or perceptual framework emerges from finding hidden value in the depths.

Aphrodite is a numinous hypnotic reality that can spontaneously influence us consciously and unconsciously at the physical, emotional, mental and mythic level. It is a fusion — mouth to mouth, heart to heart, body in body and soul in soul.

Primordial wisdom tells us that mankind can participate in the sacred during physical sexual union.

The way of the couple, mutual affection, unites not only physical and material lives in partnership, but sensation, emotional intimacy, and aesthetic tastes. Sharing intellectual interests, enrichment, and spiritual discoveries unite the lovers who grow together with one another on all planes of aspiration.

We can imagine Aphrodite much more broadly as the relativity of all psychological phenomena and symbolic imagination. Psyche and soma are joined by the bridge of imagination. In the phenomenological view, symbols emerge from human engagement with the social and material environment just as psychic life emerges from embodied action in the world.

Soulwork is the art of living soulfully and fully embodied, consciously aware of the depth dimension and its interaction with our body, emotions, mind, and spirituality. Through myth we participate in our own transcendence. Aphrodite's way is a soul-centered, open-hearted way of being. The dreamy nature of love is symbolically retained in her fluidity, meter, and rhyme.

She is the extroverted world of sense and sensuality and the immanent world of imagination. Stimulating the imagination is erotic. We carefully take hold of our experiences with enough passion and loyalty to hang onto and continue them through the multidimensional layers of meaning Aphrodite imposes on reality.

Embodied Truth

A sense of meeting in the imagination arises, revealing the dual structure of individuality, otherwise unknowable. This mighty source of psychic energy fuels imagination to create a field of inner freedom and curatorial narrative. Narratives, both personal and collective, arise from the desire to have life display coherence, integrity, fullness, disclosure, and closure.

Aphrodite is an embodiment of the non-rational and psychological union of opposites wherein the lovers are annihilated. Her form is ecstatic, reconciling. Opposite principles are brought together by desire. A similar union of opposites, the alchemist and *soror mystica*, is the goal of alchemy — deep union with the divine and feminine principle that opens our senses and reconnects us with the body. This is the spirituality of earth, life, and the present moment.

Images can ignite angelic and carnal pleasure in us as much or more than any mortal human. A 'Venus in Fur' evokes the paradox of refined animality, perhaps dangerous, sly, even deranged. Ideally, we see Aphrodite's beauty in every thing, person, and event in the world. It is there, whether we refine our perceptions to see it or not. We cannot blind ourselves to her continuous revelation — nature's unfurling dance of the seven veils.

Through the mystique of the non-rational, we cultivate life through acts of love. She renews awareness of the importance of a certain kind of sexual ritual and liminal transformative space where the unconscious manifests and opposites reconcile. With cooperation and mutuality between the sexes, each act becomes one of gender reunion, rather than power and domination from either side. The 'hermaphrodite' is born.

As a cosmic factor, she is the very essence of existence. But as a complex and paradoxical goddess, she also wounds the heart and soul. She may be the great brightness of the dawning light as inner gold. Only the awakened are truly immortal.

But she is also the material opaqueness of darkness, instincts, feelings, and raw emotions. Emotions are repetitive thoughts packed with intensity. She symbolizes the spiritual and physical duality of humanity, and all the frightening prospects of love gone wrong — devastation, disconsolation, and despondency, even revenge of the raging heart. She can be as repulsive as beautiful. Spiritual love counters the unbridled power of attraction.

When the irresistible desire for union takes precedence, Aphrodite is there. The drive — the living Presence — may be sexual, but the impulses and non-rational urges can be psychological and even spiritual. Intercourse is her epiphany, and the more planes of mind, heart, and spirit that are penetrated, the fuller the ravishment of union. Such feelings can exalt even mundane sex.

The heart wants what it wants and actively and spontaneously initiates interaction. We do it and may objectively watch ourselves in that flow of passion at the same time, in awe and wonder at its power over our rational being. It makes us think and do things we never would otherwise. It is not without reason that we call it 'falling' in love. Whatever gods have been in charge of our attitudes and lives are toppled when Aphrodite is in ascendance.

The Universal Medicine

Love is a psychedelic state, effecting rebirth — a new form, rejuvenation, immersion in the creative energy flow. Instinctual attraction dissolves the ego and liquifies consciousness in a new incarnation of spirit. Something in us dies if we don't periodically resonate with wild rejuvenating nature and meaningful ecstatic involvement.

Rebirth typically opens us to the transpersonal domain with its virtually infinite creativity, but not without the implied dissolution, death itself from which that rebirth is coming. Being in the physical-symbolic means internally and externally hearing the breath of the spirit in dialogue with the soul, with the *anima mundi*.

How have your attitudes toward sexuality changed over different periods in your life?

Consider your first time, love at first sight, addictive, illicit and forbidden love, rejection and lost love, vanities, romantic idealism and follies, sexual fantasies, inner partners, devotional and exploitive relationships. Escapism, inspiration, and all forms of artistic creativity can be associated with the generative power of luminescent Aphrodite.

This powerful archetypal theme is initiatory in character. The process of rebirth is the mythic enactment of "the one story," whose pattern is found in every narrative. Beneath the differences, the meaning — having to do with the loss and recovery of identity — does not change. The descent, including 'falling in love' with a subsequent ascent, means going deep into the consciousness journey and emerging transformed.

Celebrating the Golden One:
Aphrodite, Oshun, and Alchemy

by Leni Hester

For many years, I have been a devotee of the beautiful Oshun, the alluring Orisa of sweet water and sexuality. Working in the context of Lukumi, an AfroCuban path derived from the Yoruba traditions of present-day Nigeria in west Africa, Oshun came and transformed my life from bottom to top, not least of which was a radical re-ordering of my relational and sexual life. Decades later, despite all the training and study I have done, all the rituals in all the different sacro-magickal contexts I have seen, my love and devotion to the Daughter of Promise remains central to my mundane and spiritual life.

What I soon discovered was that many women I knew had similar experiences with their patron Goddesses, who was almost invariably Aphrodite. I began to notice many resonances between them that opened up my understanding of both.

Hard polytheism notwithstanding, there is an unfortunate tendency to lump deities with similar aspects and powers together, as being the "same." This was certainly said to me on a number of occasions, that Oshun was "Aphrodite with a tan," that she was identical with her and that they could stand in for each other. Moreover, the same could be said for any of the planetary love-n-sex Goddesses, so that Venus, Ishtar, Freya, Isis, et cetera were all essentially the same, with minor variations in dress and climate. Putting aside all the many, many ways this statement is wrong, it is also absolutely counter to my experience, and to the experiences of women and men who are intimately involved with either or both of these Goddesses.

However, it is impossible *not* to notice the resonances and similarities between Oshun and Aphrodite, in their manifestations, their powers, and their magick. They both manifest as beautiful, alluring women, seductive, sexual, luxurious, infinitely desirable. They are both associated with water — Oshun with rivers, and Aphrodite with the sea. They both are associated with flowers: one of Aphrodite's epithets is Antheia, "friend of flowers," while Oshun has strong associations with flowers and pollinators. But perhaps the most telling similarity is their affinity for precious metals. Gold, copper, even brass — the power of precious metal is both literal and metaphoric.

Oshun's connections to precious metals is well documented in both lore and history. In West Africa, the Goddess is associated with all forms of wealth — whether in the form of gold, honey, or children — and ornamentation. To display one's wealth in the form of gold and brass jewelry was to embody her queenly grace. When Oshun was brought to the Americas via the mechanism of the Transatlantic slave trade, these connections continued. Even today, those initiated into Lukumi receive five gold bangles to wear in her honor. Traditionally, these were also made of brass or copper. In creating her altars and shrines, and preparing her offerings, gold is everywhere

Gold is also associated with Aphrodite. In *The Goddess Path,* Patricia Monaghan writes that, of all the symbols associated with the Goddess, "… the one most consistently associated with her is gold — not just the yellow metal but gold as a quality of light. She is often called 'the golden one' or simply 'the golden.' … Golden neckbands and rings are beautiful, and she is always described and depicted as wearing golden jewelry" (Monaghan, 95). Again, beautiful jewelry adorns and magnifies the beauty and feminine grace of the Goddess. But is there something deeper than mere ornamentation at work here?

The effect of these Goddesses upon the lives of their devotees is profound. Traditionally, those who kept their temples and practiced the sacred rites of either of these divine energies made staggering sacrifices to do so. In modern times, the arrival of these Goddesses will cause transformation that can be startling in its speed, its reach, and its implacability. It is not for the faint of heart, but engaging either Aphrodite or Oshun will cause changes to begin. All forms of dysfunction will begin to rankle; all compromise chafe, all old grudges will either disappear or boil over with renewed force. Every obstacle to full expression and authenticity will be rooted out. In this sense, the gold these Goddesses bring is the alchemical process of change.

The fertilization of an egg, the pollination of flowers, the attraction of the lover to the beloved, the process of the human soul struggling with its woundedness and arriving at deeper empathy — all of these are essentially alchemical processes, in which the dross of base matter is acted upon and new worlds are created as purest gold is brought out of the change. Aphrodite's alchemical significance is both in the desired outcome — gold — and in the process itself, symbolized by copper, a highly conductive metal that has long been associated with Venus. Both Oshun and Aphrodite rule the experience of love, all forms of love, but more importantly they rule that part of love that changes us profoundly, that compels us to be better than we were, to love more than we did. To be changed for the better by love. In this way, these Goddesses operate powerfully as alchemical deities, transformative deities.

There is no greater power than that of love, and in tapping into Aphrodite's power, we see this power acting through us, in our own lives, and radiating out, to improve the lives of the people we love and connect with most.

Dedication to Aphrodite and Eros

by Shauna Aura Knight

I hadn't ever planned to dedicate myself to Aphrodite, but much to my surprise, this became a powerful relationship that stunned me. It was a dedication to Aphrodite, to Desire. To Wanting. In 2006, I was in my second year of training at the Diana's Grove Mystery School. Each year, we'd work with a myth or fairy tale, and that year we were working with the story of Psyche and Eros.

Over the years, my spiritual practice has moved from vaguely polytheistic to a more pantheistic worldview. During my time at Diana's Grove I was somewhere between polytheism and pantheism. One of the techniques we used at this mystery school was dedicating to an element, or to one of the deities or characters from that year's stories.

The practice allowed us — whether we worked with them as deities, spirits, or as archetypes — to deepen our connection to some aspect of that element, deities, spirits, or archetypes.

My mentors had a habit of retelling stories, especially working to tell the "villain's" side of the story. Aphrodite is usually painted as the jealous Mother-In-Law who tries to thwart Psyche's attempts to be with Eros. My mentors posed the idea that it was somewhat ridiculous that the

Goddess of all Love and Desire would actually feel threatened by a mortal girl, no matter how beautiful. What if, instead, Aphrodite's love for her son Eros, and by extension for Psyche, was so great that she was willing to test Psyche, to challenge her, so that Psyche could step beyond her mortal self in order to become a goddess? Only in becoming a goddess would Psyche be able to be with Eros. And the only way to do this was for Psyche to go through the hero's journey to become more than she was.

That was the setup for the work of that year's Mystery School, and the version of Aphrodite I dedicated myself to for the year.

Why Aphrodite?

While each participant in the mystery school would find themselves in the role of Psyche during the course of the year, I specifically found myself choosing to dedicate to Aphrodite. I chose Desire. When I think back, I realize there really wasn't any other choice for me, given the strange twists and turns of my own life.

I had been laid off from my job in the middle of 2004. Not long after that I attended my first Witch Camp at Diana's Grove, and I signed up for the Diana's Grove Mystery School in 2005. In early 2005 I began attending weekend intensives, and soon after I was building a shrine to Brigid in a grove of trees on the land. It was during that time, and after coming out of a deep depression, that I realized I wasn't happy in my marriage at all. My husband wasn't a bad guy, but I wasn't in love with him, and our lives had been diverging for a long time.

In a massive leap of faith, I left my husband and moved to Diana's Grove to follow my spiritual calling. I did what terrified me and upended my entire life. I dove headlong into the personal growth work and the leadership training. If I hadn't already lost my job, I might not have been quite so willing to turn my whole life upside-down to do that work. I sacrificed stability, I sacrificed living in the city in a place that I knew, and I sacrificed the emerging friendships I'd been building with people connected to the Reclaiming group in Chicago. I sacrificed a marriage which, though lacking in passion, was at least safe.

And somewhere in there I fell in love. I fell in love with my spiritual calling to serve, and I fell in love with the work of Diana's Grove, I fell in love with a guy. It was a trifecta of love and lust and passion. The lack of a Happily Ever After taught me a lot about desire.

Frozen Over

I have often been somewhat lacking in desire and passion. In middle-school, to cope with the bullying, I had a mantra that I learned from the movie the Terminator. The character Kyle Reese says, "Pain can be controlled, you just disconnect it." I'd say that over and over. *Pain can be controlled.*

Freezing my emotions over kept me safe and sane while growing up. As an adult, though, once I started wanting to actually feel emotions, it wasn't as easy as just turning it back on. My mom jokingly calls me Mr. Spock for my Vulcan-like approach to emotions. In relationships, however, I've noticed the strain. Men want emotions from me that I sometimes just don't have.

It's worth acknowledging that my romantic partners always eventually take second string to any creative project I've been involved in, and they grow to resent that too. At first, they fall in love with my passion for my artwork, my writing, my event planning projects. Later, they want to know why I don't love them as much as I love my work. I suppose it's always been easier for me to emotionally connect to a project, to a painting, to a creative act, than to a relationship, but even that is oversimplifying my relationship to desire and to passion.

When I fell in love in the midst of upending my life, my heart was cracked open. I don't think I even realized how much I was actually feeling until my heart was broken.

There are a lot of ways to break a heart beyond the obvious romantic scenario. There's unrequited love, of course. There's also betrayal by a friend, or an organization falling apart, or a leader falling off their pedestal. There are a host of other reasons and they can all interweave. Having opened my heart, having desired and reached, and having been denied, it doesn't really matter whether the heartbreak came from a lover or a group or a project.

There was a night when I sat out in a warm summer rain crying until I had dry heaves. It's been long enough since that night that I can acknowledge I was full of a lot of self pity and "why me." However, I'd done so much sincere personal work to unfreeze my heart so I could feel … I'd taken so many risks to open up … to try new things … it was almost more than I could bear in that moment to be denied and rejected. To be hurt like that felt like such a betrayal. I felt that the gods had led me to this place, I felt that I had been called and I'd taken that leap of faith … and to have so many things fall apart felt like a tremendous betrayal.

That night was one of those moments on the knife's edge of my own destiny. It changed everything for me.

Desire

Months later, I dedicated to Aphrodite and to Desire. After such hurt, it felt like a risk. And yet at that point, I suppose I felt that the only way out was through. I was committed to a path of personal growth, and obviously I needed to understand something more about love and desire. I was no longer naïve enough to think that it was always going to work out; indeed, I knew by that point that the path of personal transformation is like a sword on the forge, being beaten and heated and shaped until all the dross is hammered out.

That year, I remember attending a workshop on charisma and enchanting a group. Even attending that workshop felt like a risk for me. I'd always identified as the loner, the person who was awkward and had poor social skills, the person who was terrible at public speaking. During that workshop, I remember someone saying something like, "Charisma is daring to be beautiful and luscious and desirable." That sat with me for quite some time.

A lot of my personal growth work, particularly at that time, was me dealing with issues of body image and shame. Growing up, I was the fat kid with acne. "Beautiful" wasn't a word I had ever associated with myself, much less luscious or desirable. In fact, I'm ashamed to admit that a large reason I married my husband in my twenties is because I had the mindset of, "Well, we get along really well, and it's not like anyone else will ever want me." It wasn't a conscious thought, but that's about where my self esteem was at.

At the time, I had lost a lot of weight, but I was still fat by the dominant culture's standards. And being rejected by the object of my desire hadn't exactly instilled me with confidence in my attractiveness.

But once again, it was a deeper desire that won out.

See, the happiest moments in my life are when I've envisioned this huge, seemingly impossible thing, and then I've figured out a way to do that thing. I've wanted it so badly that my desire lit me up, filled me with the fire and the ability to do the thing, or to motivate a team to do it and manifest that vision.

And I wanted that. I wanted to be able to inspire people, to be the charismatic leader and teacher that could serve communities and make amazing things happen. There was a moment where I cracked once again, where I realized, I couldn't do what I was called to do by being the loner in the corner who wore a lot of black and wasn't comfortable talking to people. I couldn't do the things I dreamed of unless I was willing to give up the awkwardness, the standoffishness, my preference for being the behind-the-scenes. I couldn't do these things unless I was willing to be visible. To be beautiful. To be desirable.

For so long, I had identified only with the moon, with nighttime, with being the quiet person in the corner. With being the rebel and the reject, the one who didn't belong.

Aphrodite tempted me out into the sunlight.

Bringing the Gold

People used to tease me about wearing a lot of black. I had a Goth phase in college, but I was wearing black far before that. In middle school and high school, I suppose it's the go-to clothing color of choice for the rebels and the rejects. It pretty nicely says, "Fuck off, I'm different," and hopefully adds a little intimidation to ward off some of the bullying. In theory, at least.

I was genuinely sensitive to the sunlight for many years in part because of my regimen of acne medication. I'm pale to begin with, but I took the whole thing to some kind of vampiric affectation. To me, the sun represented the popular people, the normal people. Normal people wore gold jewelry. Pagans and Goths wore silver. Wearing black and connecting to the moon and to silver felt like some strange kind of rejection of the people who had rejected me.

What I've learned through years of personal growth work is that sometimes, we hold onto these little psychic life-rafts. When we're bullied and abused, we often survive by thinking that we're somehow better than our abusers, that we're perhaps meant for something greater. It might be something as silly as what clothing we wear, or pretending to be oversensitive to the sunlight, but it keeps our minds intact when we'd otherwise break. In essence, we have to believe in ourselves.

I think of it as our psyche's version of Dumbo's magic feather. Who knows what any one person will grasp onto. The challenge is that there's a time in our lives when the magic feather holds us back.

As I was doing the work to come out of my shell, there was a quiet little part of me that remembered my mom singing "You Are My Sunshine" to me as a kid. She used to call me that,

"Sunshine." In fact, my middle name "Aura" was almost my first name. A friend of hers who read auras told her that I had a golden aura *in utero*. This, for some reason, prompted my mom to paint all of my childhood furniture marigold yellow, which probably also served to propel me toward becoming a Goth in an act of rebellion against such cheery colors.

As I continued doing personal work, I spent a lot of time thinking of the sun, and of gold. I still thought of it as something that was for other people. Yet, when I moved to Diana's Grove, I was out in the sun all day, every day. I had to let go of the idea that I would somehow melt by being out in the sun for that long. I wasn't, in fact, a vampire. Did I burn? *Yes.* Did I melt? *No.*

In fact, I basked in the light, though at first I was loathe to admit it.

I had built this entire identity out of being the tough loner who didn't need anyone. *Pain can be controlled.* You can't reject me if I've already rejected you. And you can't hurt me if I don't feel anything.

And I was trying to remember that little girl I was, before the bullying started. Back when my mom called me "Sunshine" and people smiled at me just because I smiled at them. I was a charismatic, happy little kid before the bullying.

I opened back up to that sunshine, to that gold, to that desire. I was working with Aphrodite as the sea, the Grail, the deep well of emotion, but I was also working with her gold, her power, her sunlight. So much of my work to step into leadership was just becoming willing to stand and be seen.

Much as Aphrodite challenged Psyche to gather wool from the golden rams of the sun, I felt challenged to step into the sunlight.

As the year progressed, I went from being terrified to lead a workshop, to realizing that there were times where if I wasn't willing to step up and do something, it wasn't going to get done. That the desire was the fuel to make the vision manifest, and it was the fuel to get me past my fear of being seen. I learned that I can stand in sunshine, I can reach for sunlight, and that *isn't betraying the part of me that connected to the moon*. It's not betraying the me that wore black and hid in the shadows. I can be the sunshine and wear black. I can be the sunshine, and be an introvert. I can wear skirts and girly clothes without betraying my strength. I can wear bright colors. I can be both of those at once. *I can hold that paradox.*

But without my willingness to feel that desire and reach, I can't manifest my dreams.

Opening to Passion

In the years since my dedication to Aphrodite, I've worked with other goddesses of love. Freyja, Inanna, Ishtar. While my body image issues are still present, I've healed a lot of old wounds. It's hard to keep my heart open, and I've gone back and forth into and out of depression, and I still struggle to feel emotions at times.

My heart's been broken again since then in different ways. Groups breaking apart, betrayals, events that had to be cancelled at the last minute or large projects that didn't come off the way I'd hoped. And, of course, failed relationships.

Sometimes I wonder if I should just stick to creative projects as a place to fuel my passions. Maybe I don't get to settle down and get married to a life-long partner. Maybe, in following my particular spiritual and creative callings, my marriage is to my work, my art, my creative projects. I won't say that the idea of this isn't frustrating, but it's less painful than it once was, particularly now that I've opened up to so much creative inspiration in my life. I don't always feel emotions in a bodily way, but my creativity is certainly flowing and I'm inspired for the work I do. While the year I spent dedicated to Aphrodite at first felt like me trying to open up to romantic love again after heartbreak, it really became about me opening up to desire, to sunlight, to being willing to be visible so that I could effectively step into leadership and public speaking.

Aphrodite Initiator

Aphrodite, for me, will always feel like the initiator that loves me enough to challenge me. That loves me enough to break my heart. That loves me enough to say, "Yes, you fell in love with this, and you can't have it. You can't have everything you want. And yet, will you still reach? Will you still desire?"

Sometimes, desire hurts.

Sometimes it hurts to want something, to be filled with such desire and know *I may not achieve what I'm reaching for.* And yet, it is through challenge that we grow. The hero's journey is a series of tests and trials that transforms the hero into the person who can do more than who they were when they began.

While I committed to Aphrodite under the auspices of opening up to romantic love, what I gained was the willingness to take the risk. And it's not that I always succeed. Sometimes I facilitate rituals that flop. Sometimes I plan events that don't go well. Sometimes I submit writing and artwork that is rejected for projects. And yet, in the past years, I've been willing to put my writing and artwork out there in a way I never have before.

Without the risk, there's no success. But being willing to risk opened me up to my own desire.

Claiming the Desire

Often people ask me how I got good at doing ritual, and how they can get better at leading rituals. And I can teach techniques of facilitation, sure. I can talk about leadership, I can talk about public speaking, I can talk about the process of a ritual and how to manage logistics. But what it really comes down to is *the desire.*

Do you desire bringing an amazing, transformative experience to your group? Are you willing to get out in front of a group of people and risk looking stupid? Are you willing to sing a chant while people stare at you in silence? Are you willing to be so filled up with energy and life force that people are willing to step past their own comfort zones in order to sing and dance and join in?

Are you willing to spend hours and hours and hours practicing facilitation by leading workshops, taking supporting roles, by learning and making mistakes?

You have to *want it.* You have to want it bad enough to risk screwing up. You have to want it bad enough to move past all your fears.

Whether we're talking about taking the risk to be a better public speaker, or be a better writer, be a better leader, or any other endeavor, we're talking about practicing till you have calluses. We're talking about being willing to put your writing or art or projects or other work out there where people will give you feedback.

What Aphrodite asked me then, and what she asks me now, is, "Do you want it? Do you *really* want it? What are you willing to do to make it happen? *What are you willing to give up?*"

And if I want it badly enough, I let that sunshine fill me up with the desire. I want it, and I reach for it. I don't always succeed, but it doesn't stop me from reaching. If there's anything I learned from Aphrodite, it's that running away from pain and from sorrow isn't going to get me what I want. In fact, the tears in my eyes often are what let me know I'm on the right path.

What do you desire? What are you willing to risk? Are you willing to stand in the sunlight, to be luscious, beautiful, and desirable?

The Marriage of Aphrodite

by Amanda Artemisia Forrester

[Partially excerpted from the author's forthcoming book, *Journey to Olympos: A Modern Spiritual Odyssey.*]

The following tale comes to us through Homer, and it is certainly one of the most well-known of Her myths.

When Aphrodite first comes to Olympos, all the male deities fall instantly in love (or lust) with Her, and begin to bicker and fight over Her. Zeus sees the danger, and has Her quickly married off to Hephaistos, believing that will solve the problem. Hephaistos can on believe His good luck! He falls instantly in love with the beautiful Goddess. He wants to make Her happy, and He seeks to win Her over by making Her many beautiful things in His workshop.

Aphrodite, however, is not happy with Her husband, no matter how hard He tries. It was foolish of Zeus to think that the Goddess of Sex can be contained by marriage. She much prefers the handsome, macho Ares to His brother. Ares is only too happy to return Her advances. They engage in an affair for quite some time, right under Hephaistos' nose. Some of the ancient writers say that Their relationship goes on so long that the three times Aphrodite becomes pregnant by Ares,

Hephaistos thinks the children are His. It is said that all of Olympos knows of Their infidelity, except for Hephaistos, obviously, and Helios, not so obviously, as Aphrodite and Ares only meet in the dark of night.

Hephaistos finally discovers the affair when, one day, Aphrodite and Ares sleep too late, and are spotted by Helios. The All-Seeing Sun immediately goes to Hephaistos and tells Him what He has seen. Seething, Hephaistos retreats to His workshop, and plots how He can get revenge on them. He creates a net of adamant so strong it is unbreakable, and so fine it cannot be seen by the naked eye. Hephaistos gently hangs the delicate net on the bedposts. He then loudly declares that He is going on a long trip to visit some of His temples and shrines on the Isle of Lemnos.

Believing Her husband has left, Aphrodite calls to Ares to come spend the night with Her. This He does, and afterwards the lovers fall asleep in each other's arms. The invisible, enchanted net then floats down onto Them, binding the two so tightly that They cannot move.

Hephaistos jumps out and bellows for all the Gods to come see, ranting about the betrayal and shame of His wife and Her lover. All the Goddesses ignore Him and go about whatever They had been doing, but the Gods run to the scene. No matter how hard the two Deities struggle, the net of adamant holds Them fast. (I'm sure the prideful Ares hated being out of control like that!) The other Gods find it hilarious and burst into uncontrollable, mocking laughter at the lovers' embarrassment. All except Poseidon.

Poseidon thinks that this is a private matter that should be left to Ares, Aphrodite, and Her husband to solve amongst themselves. He pleads with Hephaistos to let Them go, which He begrudgingly does. He then divorces the Love Goddess on the spot.

They are both much happier after that. Aphrodite is a primordial Goddess of love, lust, beauty, and sex. Zeus's plan to tame Her through marriage to the solid and dependable Hephaistos fails miserably. Aphrodite is and always will be an independent Goddess, giving of Her sexuality and Herself freely. Loosed from Her marriage, She takes many Gods and mortals as Her lovers: Hermes, Dionysos, Poseidon, Pan, and Anchises are just some of Her conquests.

A New Interpretation

Homer's version of the marriage of Aphrodite is the most common, e.g., Aphrodite was married to Hephaistos against Her will and betrayed Him with His brother Ares. Laurelai Dabrielle, the author of *In Her Service: Reflections from a Priestess of Aphrodite*, sees the union of Aphrodite and Hephaistos differently.

I related in an earlier chapter how Dabrielle believes that Hephaistos and Athena were lovers. Her book includes two rituals, one of which contains a ritual drama in which her views about the marriage of these seemingly mismatched Gods become clear. In the play, Hephaistos confronts His wife Aphrodite, telling Her that He has heard rumors that She does not really love Him and is repulsed by His lame and twisted legs. She tells Him that Her love has been misunderstood and misinterpreted by the poets. He asks Her how She can love Him, a cripple, and She responds:

Beauty does not sit on the surface of a face or body. True beauty shines through it. Your beauty is in your imagination, your heart and your hands. Sooty and calloused as they seem, lustrous beauty shines in all they create.

I delight in your gifts and your talents. I love your capacity to love me so deeply. But until you love yourself, you deny the greatest portion of your love[15].

---

[15] Laurelai Dabrielle. *In Her Service: Reflections from a Priestess of Aphrodite.* Magic Woods Publishing. Indiana. 2007. pg 58.

Myths

Venus
by Hendrick Goltzius

Aphrodite Falls in Love

by Marc Littman

Aphrodite could have any Adonis on earth, but the Goddess of Love chose a lanky young man with high-functioning autism who knew more about Greek gods and mythology than a mere mortal should.

Jacob Bernstein was obsessed with the Greek gods and Aphrodite, in particular. An odd choice, perhaps, considering Jacob at eighteen still hadn't shed his virginity and had scant prospects. His skin was pimpled, he wore braces, his already thinning hair had the consistency of steel wool and through his pop bottle glasses Jacob saw the world through the prism of a rampant imagination whose images didn't always match reality.

"But she's real," Jacob insisted to his dubious parents. "Aphrodite was wearing her magical girdle that compelled me to fall in love with her. She tried to kiss me, and then she showed me things."

A prurient flame flickered in the eyes of Jacob's father. "I can imagine," Ross stifled a laugh as his wife elbowed his ribs.

Jacob blushed crimson.

"Not that stuff, beautiful things. She caressed my hand and suddenly we were sliding along a rainbow floating above Niagara Falls just like the mural I painted for the preschool."

Jacob's mother, Esther, whispered conspiratorially in her husband's ear. "I think we need to adjust Jacob's meds."

Jacob appeared flummoxed. "I wasn't hallucinating! Why don't you believe me?!"

Ross adjusted the sails of logic and tried to steer his son's ship back to reality.

"Why would the Goddess of Love fall for you, Jacob, when she could have any lover, mortal or immortal?"

Jacob scrubbed the bristle sprouting on his chin. "Well, Zeus, fearing the other gods would fight over Aphrodite, married her to crippled Hephaestus, the God of fire, a blacksmith that hammered magnificent armor and weapons for the Olympians. Hephaestus was ugly, like me."

"You're not ugly." Esther reached to comfort Jacob, but he eluded his mother's arms.

"I know what I am. But Aphrodite didn't care. She whisked me across the ocean, and we soared with pelicans just beneath the curl of a wave until we landed on the island of Cyprus. We then rode horses to a craggy overlook where Aphrodite pointed out how she came ashore on a giant scallop. She rose from the sea foam after the Titan Cronus castrated his father Uranus and dumped his genitals in the sea, delivering beauty from tragedy."

"All this in a day?" Ross tossed his son another lifeline, but Jacob swam away.

"And then we were back in St. Paul and a violinist playing outside a bookstore beckoned us.

Aphrodite removed my glasses and I could see the notes she was playing and I traced the swirls with my fingers. I tipped her the ten bucks our neighbor Bob insisted I take for shoveling his driveway's snow. We meandered to the park where a grandmother was playing peekaboo with her baby granddaughter. I laughed as hummingbirds and doves fluttered in our hair. I breathed in the sweet scent of the warm sea."

"In Minnesota? In the winter?" Ross tried another tactic.

This time Jacob docked.

"Guess I was tripping after all." Jacob's weary head fell on his chest.

"Should've let her kiss you." Ross patted Jacob's shoulders as the youth slunk to his bedroom. There Jacob lay on his bed, staring up at the ceiling picture of Aphrodite that he had lovingly drawn. Tears welled in his rheumy eyes.

"You don't have to be beautiful to appreciate beauty," Jacob mused.

"And maybe beauty is what you see within and without," a dulcet voice sang in Jacob's head and echoed joyfully through his body.

Jacob turned to face the frosted bedroom window and Aphrodite's reflection warmed the pane. And this time Jacob let the Goddess of Love kiss him, and he kissed her back.

Becoming a Priestess of Aphrodite

by Jinny Webber

In my former life I was called Teiresias, attendant on King Labdacus of Thebes.

The night my wife died in childbirth, I lost that self in a passion of grief and guilt. How could I continue in our house alone? How would I cope with a shrieking newborn and her benumbed two-year-old sister? I owed it to their mother, now so cold, but I simply couldn't.

At dawn I stumbled out the door, leaving my daughters in the nurse's charge. In a sleepwalker's trance I slipped through Thebes' gate, cutting through fields, noticing nothing until I found myself walking on leaves and pine needles beyond all human path. Sticky webs brushed my face, caught in my hair; branches pushed against me. I swept them aside with my staff and walked on, heedless of where I was.

Chill silent air shocked me into alertness. No path before or behind me, only leafy mold under my sandals, stunted growth beneath dusky pines and alders.

An other-worldly smell came to me, raising the hairs on my neck. My breath shallow, feet leaden, I could see nothing, shadow-blinded. At my feet a ripple of blue on copper: gnarled roots come to life. No! they were two massive serpents writhing in a primal dance of love.

I stood suspended, my staff poised above the serpents who seemed to consume each other. All certainties left me — of self, of body, of Teiresias, civic man and knowing mind. At this twilit still moment, I could have been the first human formed from damp red soil by the Great Mother, newborn, fearful. The serpents in their eerie coupling were the essence of all beyond human ken, paralyzing me except for a small fire burning within.

The coppery glint of those twisting bodies ignited it into blazing manly rage and I struck. Driving my staff between the serpents with all my might, my arm and stick vibrated with the blow.

The earth shook beneath me. I staggered forward. Around me, absolute silence. My vision opened full circle, encompassing both serpents as they darted away, lithe, faster than thought, one to the east, one the west.

A film covered my eyes and I fell to the ground, encased in an unbearable tightness. I burrowed deep into pine needles and rotten leaves, into the abrading soil and pebbles and roots beneath, out of my clothes and still I pushed, as if through my very skin. The sensations exhausted me and I fell into a sleeping dream world.

A fat old woman loomed over me. "Justice strikes you for trespassing! You, mortal man, dared to wander into the Great One's garden." She pulled her robe open and laughed, huge breasts and belly shaking. A wave rippled through her, serpent undulation, and she exposed her dark triangle.

"Look. Know." She moved in an obscene dance. "See what happens when a reckless man falls into the womb cave!"

Her laughter echoed, raucous, throaty, a sharp wind rumbling the trees. My mind surfaced under the cold gray sky. I wanted to cry, "Why do you taunt me, you ribald old goddess?" But I could barely manage breath, let alone speech.

My body felt strangely light, hair falling over the arm under my head — cascades of hair. And my face — how soft the skin! Young. I pressed my eyes shut. Let this be a dream! It felt like a nightmare.

My free hand couldn't resist running down over my chest. Breasts! My waist tapered, sloping downward to a rounded mound soft with hair opening to — to woman's subtle organ. A wound. A secret. A dread metamorphosis.

My maleness had been ripped from me. I wanted to pound the betraying earth, to shout to the skies. Trespasser indeed! Step into the Mother's garden and *he* becomes *she*? My anger receded: I could not summon Teiresias's fire. I said my name, "Teiresias," in a woman's voice. My mind in a woman's body! Then — could I call it my mind? So it still seemed, yet I was no Teiresias.

Sitting in the mud among twisted roots and decayed leaves, I could only laugh aloud and throw the Great Goddess a kiss. *Your serpents caught me. The Trespasser.*

I'd fallen into the void, to freedom, Teiresias' burdens lifted, all potential before me. Nothing to do but surrender. Dazed, yet strangely acquiescent, I sat in that musky forest through the day, unable to consider my next step.

An image came into my mind at last: Thebes. Home. I stood up, shook out Teiresias's tattered robe and pulled it round me. Somehow I found the road and reached the city by moonlight, slithered through the gate and over familiar streets, unobserved.

My house was dark, cold, and quiet. I let myself into my room through the courtyard and fell into bed.

At dawn I was still — woman. In the bathing court, I splashed water on my face, used the privy squatting as my wife Chloris had. No maintaining dignity. I stared down at myself, at my neat downy triangle and shuddered. The eyes that looked back at me from Chloris's hand mirror were Teiresias's, gold-flecked brown, framed in matted blond hair around a strange woman's face. I ran a comb through the snarls, managing to smooth the top layer, and put on a long heavy-textured robe, tying a cord around my waist.

At the door of Chloris's empty chamber, I gazed at the bed where she had lain, where I held her in hopeless farewell. During my absence, her funeral rites had begun — and finished? I shook my head to dispel Artemis' condemning voice. I did not risk disturbing the nurse and babies in the adjoining nursery.

On Chloris' table a long shawl woven in a blue serpentine pattern gleamed like a gift. Under the blue shawl lay a golden girdle, as intricately designed as the one encircling Aphrodite's waist, the goddess's mythic girdle that makes her irresistible to god and man. I fit it around my waist.

Never did I see such a girdle on Chloris, not even before pregnancy swelled her belly. Adorned in a girdle like Aphrodite's own, I heard the love goddess laugh my name into my ear. *Teira*. Tears and laughter. Aphrodite's Teira.

And so shall it be told as long as tales are heard: Teiresias struck apart two serpents coupling in the deep woods and became woman — and priestess of Aphrodite.

I found my way to the shrine of Mydon, the Serpent Priest of Thebes, a man Teiresias had scorned — indeed suspected of loving Chloris. But now I needed his wisdom.

Mydon gave me a gold serpent ring and told me that my destiny was Corinth, Aphrodite's mystic city, a long walk south. The very name, Corinth, emanated a cloud of perfume like that of the goddess' enchanting girdle or Hephaestos' golden filigree net which snagged her in bed with her lover Ares. Where better to be serpent priestess than to live among the most beautiful women in all of Hellas, priestesses ruled by no man, neither divine nor mortal? I would go to the temple of Aphrodite on the Acrocorinth, city of excess, her port bringing riches and worshippers from all the world.

Imagined flutes summoned me; tambourines, intoxicating fragrances, seductive laughter. I shed my Theban skin and departed my sad manly homeland, praying for Aphrodite's protection.

My safety on the road came from priestesses in woodland sanctuaries, women descended from those who fled Crete after the cataclysm destroyed their temples and shrines, women whose existence Teiresias had never even imagined. They comforted me, fed me, allowed me to sleep in their sacred domains.

As I approached Corinth, the sunbaked road grew wider and busier, but in the bustle no one noted me, though I covertly examined each as he passed by. My brief life as woman seemed very private amidst this crush of farmers and peddlers and pilgrims, and I wondered if I knew enough to survive here.

Late in the day I saw the outlines of Corinth against a distant hill. Coming close enough to make out its ochre wall and buildings, I found a smaller path and climbed a low hill overlooking the gulf, deep azure in the afternoon light. The climb became steep and rocky before I reached a wide bluff with a few windblown trees, tamarisk bushes, and a cave opening into the hillside.

A woman came towards me: Carpho, priestess to Demeter, she called herself. Her face was sunburnt and leathery, her body and manner more those of farmer than priestess: bare muscular arms and sturdy legs under a shift which she'd hiked into her belt.

"This seems a desolate place. Many come here to be alone, however, so I rarely am. You are welcome, child." Carpho offered me cherries from a basket. "That girdle of yours is a gift from Aphrodite, is it not?"

I shrug a nod. "Can you tell what awaits me in Corinth?"

"You have a rare history, a rare destiny. Beautiful women wearing a sign from Aphrodite often come to Corinth. Go to her temple and join in the dance."

"Do you know my history?"

She studied my serpent ring. "I know that you will learn more than other women here. Trust your vulva, trust your destiny." At my startled expression she laughed a quick snort then continued, "You have no secrets from me, my girl. You shall do well; never fear. Do you see Aphrodite's temple on top of the Acrocorinth?"

I followed her pointing finger until I made out a structure that had blended in with the rocky hilltop in my dazzled vision.

"That is your destination — tomorrow. Remain here tonight."

Carpho poured us each a cup of wine from an earthen jar. Even well-watered, the wine felt strong to my travel-lightened stomach.

The sun set over Corinth, filling the sky with brilliant rose and aqua reflected in the wind-roughened bay. Carpho set out barley-meal bread and goats' cheese and the basket of cherries, to me after my long trek, a feast. "In the morning someone will come to accompany you to the city." We ate in silence, reflecting on the splendor spread out below us and, to me, the mysteries of the hill above.

Carpho refilled our cups. "Your ring is older than I am. Nothing like it is made today; it holds great power. The serpent twines through all existence. We shed the old to be reborn, and reborn again."

The moon rose, coldly distant. "Sleep under these trees, Teira. I keep long vigil, but you, I see, are tired." I felt my exhaustion and would have welcomed a bath.

She smiled as if reading my thoughts. "It's dry on this hill, but two springs flow in Corinth. The fountain outside the city gates is called Peirene Cenchrias, to honor the tears of the mother of Cenchrias, spotted serpent lad mistakenly killed by Artemis. You may wash yourself there. When you climb to Aphrodite's temple high on the Acrocorinth, you will find the eternal spring Peirene, created when the winged horse Pegasus struck his hoof against the rock. The city and the temple are enriched by its unfailing waters. Drink of sacred Peirene before you enter the temple."

As I drifted toward sleep, I heard Carpho murmuring the story of the city, how it was founded by the scoundrel Sisyphos, who won no love from his fellows but established Corinth as a center of navigation and trade. How its history reflects the fate of its founder, now perpetually pushing his heavy stone in Hades for trying to trick even the gods. How Bellerophon bridled Pegasus on the Acrocorinth, thus taming the winged son of Medusa to carry him safely through danger. How every hero has visited Corinth and always will, his life forever changed. How women there, when blessed by the goddess, can gain rare stature as priestesses in Aphrodite's temple.

My dreams were filled with images of Corinth, many times more splendid than familiar Thebes; more exciting and frightening, full of adventure and threat and promise. Its soft ocher stones appeared gold, its springs and fountains flowed exuberantly.

In the morning Carpho and I walked to a patch of tilled soil where we tended her vegetable patch. "Last night you told me stories of Corinth that filled my dreams with wondrous images."

"You shall know its opulence and its shadows, more than dreams can tell," she said.

"Do you never visit the city?"

"Only if I am called. It's enough to watch its distant walls through the changing light each day."

I sat on a rock facing the gulf and the isthmus which cut through to the Saronic sea. Two great ships moved toward the port. Red and white sails arced over blue-black water; shimmers of heat made the air sparkle and my spirits with it.   A goatherd climbed the hill towards us.

"Go your way, my child. Don't forget—"

I thought she would say "me" and reached to give her a daughterly embrace.

"—to laugh!" She hugged me and waved her short skirts in farewell, the goatherd too slow-moving to catch a view.

He made a curt bow, set his milk jugs on a flat rock, picked up her empty ones, and headed back down the path.

"I shan't forget. Thank you, Carpho!" I called as I ran after him. Just once he turned to offer his hand over treacherous rocks. As we approached the long city walls, he waved me in the direction of the Peirenean fountain of Cenchrias and turned away. Was he mute? Never mind. No one need point out the temple queening above the city.

I joined a group of women at the fountain, splashing its water over my face and hair and arms, which earned me alarmed looks from the women as if to ask, whoever is this barbarian?

The sun warm upon me, I followed those walking into the city. An old man gave me figs, and I savored their sweet seedy meat as I walked through the busy streets. The road sloped upward, away from houses and shops to the long climb to the temple. I was relieved when the path wound into the shade. Worshippers of Aphrodite must be hardy of limb and breath, I thought, as I stopped to rest.

At last the path widened towards Aphrodite's temple, colossal, as if gods or giants had dropped its huge stones from heaven in perfect symmetry to honor their darling. Not only did the temple look out upon gulf, isthmus, and bay, but its perspective stretched far to the south, over the vineyards and orchards of the vast Peloponnese. I inhaled the tangy air that soon would become my life breath, an unforgettable mingling of sea and lemon blossom, rockrose and anise.

Remembering Carpho's instructions to visit the spring, I circled the wide tiled steps at the front, allowing myself only a glance at the large statue of Aphrodite inside, glittering with jewels. An empty courtyard extended from the back steps to a low building with a trellised entry. Voices sounded from within, but no one appeared. By the stone steps, I found the sacred Peirenean spring and filled my hands to drink again and again, in thirst and in prayer. To success in Corinth!

The spring gushed out of a deep cleft in the rocks where it had been struck by the hoof of Pegasus, sudden, like Teiresias' staff between the serpents — though to my fresh eyes, it appeared like the waters of life pouring from the body of the Great Mother herself.

We're told that the winged steed Pegasus was born from Medusa's neck when Perseus struck off her snake-curling head. Poor Medusa: her lovely hair was her undoing. Sea-lord Poseidon, entranced, ravished her within Athena's temple when she came to make her devotions.

I recalled such stories from the palace of King Labdacus, recalled Teiresias's amusement at the gods' ingenious and insatiable seductions and his horror at the monstrous Medusa who challenged Perseus to heroic victory. Now I pitied the girl Medusa, punished by Athena for the sacrilege which she did not commit — raped, not seduced — her flowing curls become snakes, her beautiful face a curse, turning to stone whoever looked upon her.

Medusa, Gorgon: and mortal, Perseus cutting off her terrifying and terrified head, avoiding her fatal gaze by looking upon her reflection in his shield. Medusa, Gorgon: immortal, for the child of Poseidon in her womb burst from her neck as winged Pegasus. The blood from her severed head, now the weapon of Perseus, dripped on land and sea to create worms and snakes and coral. Why a winged horse? Why life from serpent blood?

Ah but here am I, a woman created from serpents. I reflected on how I'd been mothered by Aphrodite in my dreams and by Carpho at her cave. And Medusa too? I smiled at a notion so impossible to Teiresias. Now the story of Medusa meant more to me than to him. Did I stand on the opposite line, the other side of the battle, man's view become woman's? Was there indeed a battle between woman and man, goddess and god?

Not in the realm of Aphrodite, born of the sea foam. Goddess of love in all its convolutions. Deny her power and be destroyed, the stories tell us. But I was here to become a human embodiment of her power, a woman touched by her divine hand.

At twilight, torches began to light the city below. Flute music called from the temple. I followed at some distance the line of women walking out of the low building, their sheer gold-hemmed gowns revealing limbs of grace and perfection as they danced toward bejeweled Aphrodite in her majesty. Torchlight played on the tile floor of the temple, its design of blue and gold imitating the sea from which Aphrodite emerged, the sea below the city, and the most beautiful of fabrics, gold-streaked gossamer. I removed my sandals and approached the towering statue of the goddess.

Imagining my blue serpent-weaving from Delphi to be a silken veil, I held it, arms outstretched, then let it accentuate my movements as I began to dance as Aphrodite taught me in my dreams, circling slowly to plaintive flute song. When a drumbeat pushed me toward a final rapid whirling, the shawl clung to my body and I fell to the ground.

Silence. I lay in front of the snake-entwined pedestal of the goddess. As I rose to my feet, I inhaled Aphrodite's grace. I turned to the women, and one, a vision of roundness under her soft peplos, stepped forward and welcomed me to the temple.

The flute resumed its slow melody and as the sinuous women moved together, I joined their line, following them out of the temple and down the back stairs. Under the trellised arbor opposite the spring stood the carved door of the long building, its shadowy images adding to my suspense. A cat sat at the marble threshold, her tawny eyes upon me. I stared back, took a deep breath, and stepped into the large central room.

Lamps flickered down a table set with platters of fruit, olives, cheese, and breads. The priestess who welcomed me, Iole, invited me to supper, saying that the women dined alone that night, entertaining no worshipers because it was Corinth's feast of Bellerophon. Everything about Iole was round, just short of plumpness: her face with its cap of dark curls becoming ringlets down her back, her black eyes, her heart-shaped mouth; her generous round breasts, arms that tapered to dimpled elbows, and beneath her tunic, curves of belly and thigh and rump. It was all I could do to keep myself from embracing her on the spot.

An attendant poured wine weaker than Carpho's, and the talk was soft and laughing. Iole sat to my right and introduced me to the priestesses around the table. Each seemed more lovely than the last, though wearing few jewels and made up only with dark outlines around their eyes. I especially noticed Polydora, tall and dark with regal bearing, and a slender girl called Calyce, coppery gold curls springing under a brightly woven band. Just saying her name now, Calyce, brushes me with delight, like a kiss on a nipple.

Iole pointed out the priestess' rooms behind tapestried draperies down each side wall. Too intrigued to eat, I managed to drink two or three goblets of wine.

The aromas of the dining hall became overwhelming. When I arrived, a light perfume fragranced the air, but now a weight of incense and woman scent assaulted me. I slipped backwards; Iole caught me, half lifting me from my seat and guiding me through one of the tapestries into an almost dark room with a soft sleeping pallet where I immediately collapsed. "Forgive ...," I whispered as I pulled the bed robe over me.

Women's' voices lulled me from beyond the curtain. Just as I was falling to sleep, I felt a strange warmth flowing from between my legs. I sat up in horror, saw in the pale light a reddish stain spreading. Nothing to do but wad up some of the bedclothes to absorb it and let myself sleep at last.

In the morning, Iole laughed at the mess. "With that much blood, it'll be a short flow. Quite a greeting our Aphrodite has given you!" She took me through a small door to an inner courtyard. Along the wall under a shallow roof were polished metal mirrors and dressing tables covered with jars and vials of perfumes and creams and unguents, kohl and rouge; small chests with jewelry, combs, hair ornaments.

"These belong to the temple, to all of us." Iole indicated a larger chest. "Choose what you like." I selected a gown of fine saffron fabric and the only robe with purple in it.

"I'll leave you to your bath, Teira. In the morning, we take little time for jewelry or makeup, only enough to please Aphrodite in the temple dance. Afternoons we spend here, arraying ourselves to meet the worshipers. Come into the dining hall after your bath." Iole pursed her full lips into a mirror and smiled at her reflected face.

Alone, I went to the fountain at the center of the courtyard and diverted its cool water over me in the tiled bathing tub. I rubbed soap into my hair, the bubbles skimming down my body with the rinse water, their foamy traces decorating my breasts and belly. What a body for one who was sinewy Teiresias not so very long ago!

Fastening my girdle over the saffron peplos I had to laugh at myself: womanly manners and style were coming surprisingly easy. I hung delicate pendants in my ears and returned to the main hall where two attendants were setting out the morning meal.

In my room, the bloodied bedclothes were gone, my blue serpent shawl folded across the end of the bed. The chamber reflected bright sunlight angling through a small window, the design on the woven rug resembling that of the ocean tiles in the temple, pillows covered in blue and gold stacked under the window.

Iole looked in. "You seem to have everything you need — except a treasure, perhaps a filigreed lamp. Surely a worshiper will bring you one."

"Who are these worshipers?"

"Men who come to praise Aphrodite — out of devotion, out of fear, duty, perhaps curiosity. They bring us roses, fruit, fine fabrics, jewels. Whenever a rich ship lands, we're assured of barrels of wine and chests of treasures. Such is the bounty Aphrodite commands."

Iole pulled me through my tapestry-hung doorway, a design of waves and lilies, into the hall where priestesses helped themselves to fruit, bread, honey. It was strange to be in the midst of these knowing women, their voices like a melodic assembly of birds among whom I felt a scraggly raven despite my finery.

As Iole and I left the dining hall, the coppery-curled priestess Calyce joined us. "I was the most recent arrival until you came. Welcome, Teira. You know the dance well."

"I feel strange here …."

"Aphrodite makes her will known. There are of course her mystery rites." Calyce's smile was innocent and conspiratorial at the same time. "We celebrate her by dancing in the temple; there's also private worship in the intimacy of our rooms.

Tonight, if her light shines on you, you will participate in these rites."

In the temple with its holy fragrance of stone permeated with incense, we were pulled into the line of linked women before jeweled Aphrodite. First drums, then a flute, drew me into serpentine movements undulating through us, turning us into a pulsing stream, around and around the statue, stopping just short of whirling frenzy. What a morning greeting to the goddess!

We returned to the bathing courtyard, which smelled gentle and flowery after the pungency of the temple. There the ritual was indolent conversation and beautifying to the sound of Marpessa's flute. Iole began a bawdy song which everyone joined. The tamer verses went like this:

> *Blessed the man*
> *To come into the cave*
> *To lie in the furrow*
> *Of the goddess' great joy*

> *Blessed am I*
> *Possessing my flower*
> *A stream and a cavern,*
> *The goddess' great joy.*

As I stood in front of a smoky mirror trying to arrange my hair, Calyce brought ornaments to weave into it, turning the free-moving mane into a work of art, curls held by gold at each temple, plaits and ringlets looping to my shoulders. I smudged kohl under my eyes.

"No, no, no," Calyce laughed, wiping off my face and showing me how to etch the inky powder into the lining of my eyes, to spread a gold-tinted cream over my cheekbones, to rouge my lips. I chose a musky perfume oil which Calyce dotted at all the points of warmth, tickling even between my toes.

"We'll hang this amethyst between your breasts," she fastened it with a cord, "and this bracelet on your ankle." I examined my emerging self from every angle in the burnished sheen of the mirrors.

Calyce laughed, "What a vain one! You must come from a village that's never seen a mirror." She disregarded my quiet answer, "Near Thebes," and continued, "We'll go to your apartment for a moment, if you're so fond of mirrors!"

She took my hand and pulled me to my room. "Now rest back on your elbows," Calyce directed me to the bed. "Here, lift your skirt," and she aimed a hand mirror so I could see myself. "Isn't that a perfect petaled flower? Like an iris, pale pink shading to lavender. I'd like to see it blushing scarlet!"

I couldn't think about what once belonged between these legs, Teiresias' muscle-knotted legs, so curious was I at this marvelous labyrinth into dark mystery, my moonflow now a mere trace of scarlet.

"Time to hide it away," Calyce took back the mirror and rearranged my skirt, "even though I'm tempted to kiss that fresh flower." She shook her curls with a laugh which piqued my yearning. "When you dance remember your hidden flower and enjoy its warmth!" She skipped away, me following, warmed through and a little shaky.

As the sun arced downward, attendants served dates and tall goblets of lemon water before preparations began for the evening dance. Iole arranged a diaphanous purple cloth over my head and shoulders and nudged me into line.

This time we circled the temple and entered by the wide front stairs, passing the altar attended by the tall Polydora, who smiled me a welcome. This dance felt very different from the morning's. Though we moved together, we did not hold hands. Men stood beyond the altar, and the heat radiating upward from my secret flower and out from my chest surrounded them and circled back to me.

Dancing near them, I heard "the goddess's grace." A man wearing the short tunic of a warrior under a long bronze-threaded robe seemed to be addressing those words to me.

As the music rose, I felt animated by the goddess, by the man; pulled toward each in pleasing hunger. Aphrodite released me to the man, my movements now only for him. I whirled faster; he reached his arm to me, and I completed the dance winding in against his chest. Laughing, I led him out of the temple, past Peirene and over the marble threshold and past the sentinel cat, her eyes half closed, through the carved door of the priestess' building, our building, disregarding the other dancers, the music resuming behind me.

In the empty dining hall, the lamp-lit table was set with great baskets of flowers. "Some wine?" He held out goblets for me to fill, lacing in water. Drumbeats and the momentum of the dance which he so briefly joined carried us to my small chamber.

"I drink to the goddess and to your beauty, which shines with her grace." He smiled, spilling a libation before drinking deeply. I felt a wave of awkwardness. What am I doing here, with a man who could be companion to Teiresias? Teiresias had touched, been touched by, a man or two in Thebes, but there was no insistence, no intimacy. This man, Damysos, wanted more from me, *Teira*.

Was it a jest of Aphrodite, that I should lose my old Teiresias self by making love as a woman with a man who resembled him? Damysos was very like Teiresias, in his case trained as a warrior in the service of King Laertes of Ithaca, yet so unlike Teiresias as to recognize Aphrodite, to open himself to her in his dreams, and to obey those dreams. Which brought him to me, her priestess.

And such I became that night.

***

I whisper long-concealed secrets; perhaps no woman shall know such divine magic again. The sacred temple of Aphrodite has slipped to a new sort of worship since those days, crass and pecuniary in a way we priestesses never knew. When I first arrived at the goddess's temple high above Corinth, it possessed a unique purity and a primal innocence, and that spirit is now restored to me in this telling for you, my dear ones.

Cupid's Mark

by Shannon Connor Winward

On Monday, I told my mother about the strange pain between my shoulders; how it's been growing worse since the night you left.

She said, "Maybe you're growing wings."

I think she was onto something. I think maybe love is like a phantom limb — the way it aches even after it's long gone.

By Thursday, the pain had driven right through my scapula. Sometime last night, it penetrated my heart.

Now it sticks like an arrow through my left breast. I keep touching it, and touching it, thinking of you, only half-surprised to find my fingers still come back red.

Deathwatch

by Gerri Leen

It had been a long road from the House of the Lady to the house of Lord Miklos, and Tala could not remember the way back. She could barely recall the day she'd forsaken the teachings of the Goddess — teachings she had spent years learning. And for what? She'd gained nothing in that long, painful journey. She'd left the temple for the love of Miklos, a man who belonged to a woman who hated Tala with everything in her. A woman who even now, as Miklos lay on his deathbed, plotted her destruction.

Tala suspected that her own last breath would not be long after her lover's. She knew that she should flee the city while she still had the chance. But what good would fleeing do?

The temple would not take her back, not after she had abandoned the teachings of the Goddess, and she could not bring herself to leave this place while her lover still breathed, even if she had been forbidden to see him.

Tala moved to the window and looked out on Bushek, a city she had first come to love and then, ultimately, to hate. Even now, as she looked up at the shining golden walls of the Miklos's house, she could feel the city closing around her. It seemed to whisper, "You can never escape. You gave up everything, and all you have left is here, within me. When he dies, so will you."

She sought the countryside, looking past the walls, and saw the hills beckoning freedom. Somewhere, just past them, lay her home. But she hadn't been paying attention when she'd ridden away with Miklos. Had been too enamored with him — and with the love they'd made on the way — to pay attention to what roads had carried her here.

But there were other ways to find home. With her mind, she sought the lines of power underneath the earth — intending to trace them to the temple she'd grown up in, a nexus of power — but her ability, so long neglected, failed her.

She could not do even the smallest magic. Despair, never far away now, rushed in. She had abandoned the Lady, and now the Lady had abandoned her.

She tried again, concentrating the way they'd taught her in the temple, centering herself as best she could, reaching for the power all around her, grounding it in the warm, dry earth that lay below her. She breathed in and out, trying to concentrate on nothing, trying to connect with the power that had once seemed so close.

A sound in the hall snapped Tala out of her meditation. As she listened, she heard something — like a rustle of old leaves. She waited for a less innocent sound, like that of a steel sword being pulled from a leather scabbard, or the creak of armor that would mean the guards had come. But there was nothing, and she finally relaxed.

It must have been the servants, whispering among themselves. They no doubt realized her days in this house were numbered. Perhaps they'd already planned where they would seek their next employment and what of her things they might steal for themselves. She had taken little time to get to know any of them, and she knew they felt no loyalty to the lord's courtesan, their mistress of the moment. Even if her moment had lasted nearly twenty years — Miklos had never tired of her.

A louder sound in the hall interrupted her reverie. Then a knock on the door brought her to her feet. A visitor? Here? Who would be so foolish? Or perhaps it was finished: her lord was dead, and the guards had finally come for her. She listened again for metal and leather, but there was nothing.

She finally moved to the door, pulling it open slowly, wrapping as much dignity around her as she could. She would meet her fate with the regal composure of a high priestess, even if she had none of that stature here.

But the hall stood empty. Tala searched the shadows for any movement, closed her eyes and listened as hard as she could. Nothing.

She shut the door, hating that her nerves were playing tricks on her. She'd always been so calm and unflappable at the temple. Her sister priestesses had come to her when they were in trouble, seeking her out as Mother Comfort, a place to confess and be reassured. But here — here, she was the one who needed comforting.

Before she could reach the window seat, the knock came again. Tala froze; her heart began to beat madly. Then anger took over. Covering the distance quickly, she whipped open the door to find nothing again.

"Stop it," she cried out to the darkness. "I know you're there."

No one responded. She thought she felt something brush her cheek softly, heard a snatch of a long-forgotten song, and then the sensation was gone and the hall was still again. She closed the door and returned to the window seat. Leaning against the wall, she gazed out at the countryside, and a weariness filled her. She slowly let her eyes close.

She was back in the temple. And it was night, at the dark of the moon. The other maidens were sitting by the black scrying mirror, and one of them — Tala tried but failed to call up her name — looked up at her and said, "Why did you abandon us?"

"Tala? Come here, my love." Miklos's voice. As it had been when he was younger and so handsome he'd stolen the breath from her chest. She turned her back on her sisters and smiled at him.

"I love you so," he said, and as he stared at her, his flesh began to change, began to wrinkle and sag, and she felt her own begin to do the same, until she was old, older even than the oldest of the priestesses in the temple. She felt her bones start to dry out, felt as if the least movement would break her in two.

She heard her sisters crying out behind her and turned. Where there had been young women, now were only bleached bones, with a scrying mirror lying between them, reflecting nothing but blackness. Then the moon began to rise, and Tala felt her body turning back, flesh firming and limbs strong again. She glanced at the bones, but they were gone, as were the maidens, and lush women stared back at her, smiling in a knowing way. One of them held up the scrying mirror, and it reflected a full, blood-red moon.

She woke with a start, sure she'd heard another knock. Hurrying to the door, shivering a little from the imagery of the dream, she opened it and found herself face to face with a stranger, a woman ancient and bent.

"May I come in, daughter?" she asked, her voice sounding like the croak of a raven.

Tala stood aside, and the crone slowly made her way to the window. "You should have been expecting me." She turned to Tala, her face expressionless.

"Do I know you, madam?" Confused by this stranger, Tala tried to keep her voice polite. The woman was obviously crazy, but she was also very old, and deserving of respect.

"You have always known me, daughter mine. Even when you believed you'd left me behind forever, I never left you."

Tala frowned, but her voice was gentle. "I'm sorry. But I've never seen you before in my life."

The woman shook her head. Her ancient eyes glittered like crystal-laced stones in a sunlit stream. Tala's mind flashed back to the bleached bones in her dream. To the mirror reflecting the ripeness of the gravid moon.

"What is your greatest fear, child?" The woman looked around the room, seemed to eye every item of value. "You have so much, and yet, you have nothing." Her voice was neutral, as if what she said was just a fact. But her eyes glittered again, and Tala felt suspicion fill her.

"She sent you, didn't she? To torment me."

"You have grown sharp in this soft prison." The old woman looked away, and Tala thought she caught a flash of tears in her yellowed eyes. "I came to see you because you need me."

"No one here cares what I need. No one but Miklos, and he will soon be dead."

The old woman looked at Tala, her eyes profoundly sad. "Don't you remember me?" She touched Tala's cheek; her hand felt like old, scratched leather.

Tala peered intently into the lady's face. "I'm sorry. If we've met, I cannot remember you."

"We have met. But it's all right." The woman's voice held a world of forgiveness, was rich with mercy that Tala did not understand. "There is not much time left for him."

Tala turned away and began to pace the room. "Mother, I do not mean to be discourteous, but it's dangerous for you to be here." Why had she chosen to call the woman "Mother"?

"There is no danger for me, child, only for you." There was a swishing sound, as if a light breeze had blown into the room. A scent of flowers and the sea filled the space. "Do you remember me now?"

Tala turned; the old woman was gone. In her place stood a young maiden, fresh and budding with all the promise of youth. "Now, Tala, now do you remember me?" she whispered in a sweet voice, and Tala thought she heard songbirds outside her window answering the question for her.

She fell to her knees, her heart pounding in her ears, as she recognized the Goddess she'd worshiped for so long as a young woman. "Oh, great Mistress of the Night, forgive me for not recognizing you." She found herself shaking, could not meet her Goddess's eyes.

The girl moved lightly to where Tala knelt, tipped her chin up so she had to look at her. "Daughter … sister, why do you fear me so?"

Tala felt tears fill her eyes. Tears of shame that she'd abandoned her goddess. Tears of frustration that she was trapped here. Tears of loss, because she still loved the man who was leaving her to this fate.

"Child, please don't cry."

"But I left you. I forgot you. I've lost you."

"Why did you do that, my heart?"

"For the love of a man." Tala could not meet her eyes. "I left the temple because I could not have him and continue in your service."

The maiden laughed, and her laughter was somehow richer and lusher than it had been. The aroma of amber and myrrh filled the room, and the breeze that blew through was hot and humid. Tala looked up. Standing in front of her was a woman in the full ripeness of life, her body richly curved, with a look of sexual promise and experience.

"My dear child, have you forgotten I have three guises? The temple taught you of the virginal maiden and the shriveled crone, but they neglected their teaching of this aspect." The woman began to dance, and the curtains blew in the breeze, keeping time. Tala thought she saw the flowers on the windows waving in tempo, too.

Doves landed on the windowsill, their soft trill making everything seem all right.

"Mother," she breathed, and her voice seemed to be swallowed up in the overwhelming sensation of becoming. Everything was possible at this moment. Everything was about to be born.

The Goddess laughed gently. "I am all that is ripe and fertile. All that is sex and creation. I have known love, and I have given it back. I make the flowers bloom and the wheat grow and animals grow fat. I am she who is the Mother of all, and I have never left you. And you have never lost me."

She lifted Tala to her feet. "It is time for you to return to the temple. I am weary of my daughters being taught only part of the truth. Take back the knowledge you have learned from your lover, let them know that there are other paths than the ones that have been carved out for them for so many years. Tell them that the Lady loves all — the maidens, the mothers, and the crones."

She reached for Tala's hand. "It is time to go, but first we must make one stop."

Tala found herself standing next to the Goddess in her lover's chamber. She backed away. "I do not wish to."

"Nevertheless, you will." The Goddess's eyes flashed, and Tala was reminded of her own mother, when Tala had defied her.

Courtiers stood around Miklos's bed, and a doctor leaned over and gently closed Miklos's eyes. His wife, the woman who hated Tala, sat hunched over him. Her back shook with sobs, and she clenched his lifeless hand tightly between hers.

Tala felt loathing flood her. This woman had stood between her and what she wanted for so long. "She only pretends to grieve."

The Goddess looked at her sharply, and Tala felt herself flushing. Moving closer to the woman, the Goddess said, "Even though she could never give him the affection he wanted and needed from her, she did truly love him. But she let duty get in the way of true emotion, and she hated you for filling that void in his life. She hated him for having that void in the first place. And she hated herself for not being a different kind of woman." The Goddess gently ran her hand over the woman's hair, her eyes full of kindness.

Tala looked down. "I never knew. I never realized."

The Goddess beckoned for Tala to approach the bed. "Come here. None alive can see us."

Tala moved over to her side.

"Place your hands on her head."

"She would never allow that." Tala still smarted over the way this woman had shunned her whenever they'd chanced to meet, acting as if Tala was lower than the beggars that crowded the streets during the festivals.

"Do it anyway."

Tala laid her hands on the woman's head. She could feel utter despair within her — so she did grieve.

"Do you feel her pain?"

"Yes." Tala tried not to sound grudging.

The Goddess pushed her hands down harder; the woman's pain welled up inside Tala, until it was all she could feel. Loss. Grief. Loneliness that would only get worse. Jealousy — awful, seething envy of the love Miklos had borne Tala.

The Goddess let up on her. "Now, you understand."

Tala pulled her hands away. "I never meant to hurt anyone."

"I know. But you still did." She had a hand on both of them, wife and mistress linked through her. "Ask her forgiveness. And forgive her."

Tala felt a peace filling her from the Goddess's touch, wondered if Miklos's wife could feel it too. "I ask forgiveness," she murmured, "and I forgive you." The peace intensified, and Tala looked at the Goddess.

The Lady smiled back, a beautiful smile — knowing and innocent at the same time. "Now, daughter, bid your lover farewell."

Tala looked at Miklos. His body was still, but his spirit rose just above it, and his beautiful eyes were open again. He smiled at her with so much love she felt her heart catch in her throat.

"Miklos," she murmured, remembering how it felt to love him, how complete she'd felt when they were one. Remembering also the fights they'd had despite that love. The harsh words. "My love, I'm sorry."

"No need, Tala. Never any need." He grinned at her, the age-old grin that had seduced her when he'd come as a pilgrim to the temple. "I don't have much time, only enough to say goodbye to you."

She forced tears away and spoke around the lump in her throat. "May the Goddess guide your way, my love." She thought she felt the hand of the Lady on her shoulder as she said it.

She'd said it like a priestess. Like she still had a right to do that.

The Goddess's hand tightened on her, but Tala felt a surge of support, not disapproval. She was a priestess. A lifetime ago, she was.

Miklos looked at his wife. "I've already told her goodbye. I loved her, Tala. In my own way."

It hurt to hear that. But with the Goddess's hand resting on her shoulder, it felt like a truth Tala needed to hear. A painful, somewhat sad truth. But nothing to fear. Nothing to rail at.

She wanted to kiss him, but he was gone, his spirit flown.

"It's time to go, Tala."

The room shimmered and everything went black for a moment. Then the light came back, but shuttered this time, because of the forest they were standing in. Up ahead something white glimmered in a clearing, and Tala felt her heart speed up.

The Goddess gave her a little push toward it, and Tala ran as she had not done since she was a girl, and soon found herself in front of the temple she had left so many years ago. It shone white and perfect in the sunshine, more beautiful than in her memories. She heard the laughter of the girls, the low strumming of some kind of musical instrument.

"Oh," she said, feeling relief and joy fill her. "Oh, I'm home."

The Lady was suddenly by her side. "Yes, you are home, child. Now go and teach my other daughters that love and the Lady are not mutually exclusive." She leaned down and kissed Tala gently on the forehead.

Tala felt all the fears of the last days leave her, and a sense of power surged through her. A ripeness filled her, a remembrance of how it felt to love, to share the joy of flesh and passion with another. "I shall never forget, my Lady, what you have done for me."

"See that you don't." The Goddess laughed and began to dance, and as she faded away the breath of her rich laughter turned into a hot, moist breeze that caressed Tala and blew her hair free of its bounds. It cascaded around her, curling in the damp as it fell into her face.

Tala's forehead tingled where the Goddess had kissed her. She closed her eyes, breathing in the last of the breeze. It seemed to fill her with purpose.

"I will never, ever forget," she whispered, "and I will teach your daughters well." Smiling, she walked into the temple, past startled novices, who called out for her to stop.

She turned to them, a smile growing on her face. It felt different, this smile. It felt like the lush smile of the Lady.

"Show me to your high priestess."

One of the novices nodded and hurried off down the hall. Tala followed, ready to begin again in the House of the Lady.

The Folly of Tyndareus

by Merit Brokaw

"Mother, why are we here?"

"I want to see for my own eyes whether the tale I was told is true." As the beauty walked into the Spartan temple, the foundations shook in anticipation of her anger. "*So!* It is true. Tyndareus has put my statue in fetters!"

Eros scratched his head. "Why would he do something so … silly? Blasphemous? Rude?"

"It is supposed to symbolize the bonds of faithfulness that wives should show their husbands." Aphrodite spat upon the fetters. "Hear me, Gods! Those of above, those of below, and those who call Gaia home! Tyndareus shall never know faithfulness. Not in his wife, nor in his children."

The temple seemed to groan at the Lady of Love's pronouncement, longer and louder than the temple's size would suggest.

"Eros, my darling son, be an angel for me. Go. Tell Zeus of the beautiful Leda, the wife of Tyndareus. Tell him I will aid his plans. Many fates will be affected by what has happened here."

***

Leda sits in her bower, listening to the noise from her kingly husband's costumed dinner where only men and harlots are allowed. She was a bit upset by this, but was more worried that the noise would wake up her infant daughter, Klytaimnestra.

Suddenly the door was flung open. There stood her husband in his costume. As she studied him, she was amazed at how beautiful his swan costume looked and how handsome and strong he appeared. A small part of her wondered how that could be since when he left her some hours ago he had looked rather ridiculous. As he came into the room and gently closed the door, she became frightened. The man looked something like Tyndareus but yet moved differently and seemed more at peace with himself.

"Husband?"

"Shhhh. All is well, Leda. I am Tyndareus, but also more than he." The man moved closer. The movements of his hands and the feathers playing across his body were mesmerizing. Without conscious thought, she reached for him, and he took her in his arms more gently than Tyndareus ever had. "Will you lay with me, oh beautiful one? I'm of a mind to plum your treasures, but have no interest in rape no matter what the stories say about me."

"Oh, yes. Yes, my Lord. Please."

In this man's arms, Leda spent the most memorable time of her life. She had never been loved so tenderly, so strongly, and so completely in her life. She wanted the night to never end.

Suddenly, a banging was heard upon the door, a staff rapping with intent. To Leda, it sounded like doom.

"Come my Lord! Your time is at an end!"

"Aye, Hermes. I know."

"Hermes?" Leda stammered. "Who are you, my swan lover?"

"I think you know, my love. I would stay longer, but neither of our spouses would approve. You really do not want the attention of my wife. Sleep, little one." And he touched her on the forehead. As she gracefully fainted in his arms, he laid her on the bed in sweet repose. Going to the door, he looked back wistfully and then strode through it. "Let's be on our way."

***

Leda awoke to Tyndareus in his filthy, ugly costume, drunkenly pushing her legs apart. Before she could protest, he cuffed her hard across the face with one hand, while he tore her shift with his other.

"I will have you when I want and how I want. I am not only your husband, but your king. No one will gain say me."

With that he commenced with his rape of her. Something he did on a regular basis. Before tonight, she hadn't minded very much. She didn't know what it could be, what it should be between a man and a woman. But now she knew and pledged in her heart to have her revenge, the revenge of a woman and a mother.

Looking away from the beast between her legs, she saw a feather on the floor left behind by her divine lover.

Across the room, Klytaimnestra started to cry.

**

Leda swaddled up the twins, hushing and humming to keep the infants quiet. She was wearing a clean gown and smelled sweetly, fresh from a bath. A feather was plaited into her hair. Next to the boys was an eggshell, from which Polydeukes had been born. They looked so much alike, she couldn't tell them apart, though initially after their birth she could.

Kastor had been born with his arms wrapped protectively around the egg. As soon as the shell cracked open, Polydeukes quickly grew into the same size and appearance as his brother. She knew, then, that one was the son of her husband and the other the son of her lover. Tyndareus, in his arrogance, claimed otherwise, and the women who helped her deliver kept quiet about the strange birth in the face of his killing anger.

Yet a child should meet his father.

Leda was taking both boys to Zeus' temple in secrecy. She had planned on only taking Polydeukes, but the twins refused to be separated quietly. And quiet was of the essence. Tyndareus had refused to give her permission to go there, saying that a woman had no business in Zeus' temple.

Go she would, with or without his consent.

Quickly and quietly she made her way to the temple. Surprisingly, the boys stayed quiet as if they understood the need for stealth. Once inside she hurried up to the bare altar. She sat down her burden and bent to remove the blankets from the twins in order to present them to Zeus. A movement caught her eye. The altar was no longer bare. Upon it was a naked baby who appeared to be the same age as the twins.

The baby started to shiver and cry. Leda picked up the child without thinking, motherly instinct and the need for stealth guiding her actions. As the child quieted, Leda again looked at the altar. There where the child had lain was a feather, an exact match to the one in her hair.

***

Leda faced her husband, laughing scornfully. "You drunken imbecile. You drink so much and spend so much time with your whores that you are not even sure how many children you have. I gave birth to *triplets!* Two boys and one girl. Shall I remind you of their names so that you can introduce them to the family and Hestia?!

Kastor, Polydeukes and Helena. I suggest you sober up first, lest you drop one of them into the fire."

***

And so Tyndareus unknowingly raised Zeus' children along with his own. Kastor and Polydeukes became known as the Dioskouroi or Zeus' youths, a slap in the face to any proud "father." Klytaimnestra, in turn, betrayed a powerful husband in favor of her lover, thus losing Tyndareus a powerful ally. As for Helena, ahh, Helena. All know to what this child's exploits led.

All these events were set in play by the arrogance of Tyndareus, thinking he could chain Aphrodite — or any woman — to the will of man.

Who am I to know this tale which differs so greatly from what others say? At one time, I was called Leda, but you, you can call me Nemesis.

As the woman walks away, two feathers gleam, plaited into her hair.

Love's Sting

by Gerri Leen

I. The Mother

Aphrodite sat on the edge of the bed, watching as life drained out of one of her faithful, blood staining the ivory bedclothes.

The woman's husband stood shaking, still holding the knife, weeping as the woman he loved died. "Please give her back to me. I didn't mean to —"

"You did." Aphrodite stood and walked over to him. "You did mean to." She let him see her fury.

He fell to his knees, crawling toward her. "Forgive me."

"Forgive yourself." She kicked him away from her.

He apparently could not forgive himself; he plunged the knife into his chest. His death was far quicker than that of his wife, whose breaths were faint but there. Wishing she had her cousin's Persephone's touch — the kiss of death that could grant release — Aphrodite sat with the woman and held her hand until she finally started her journey to Hades' realm.

Suddenly, a great boom sounded from behind Aphrodite, and she heard warhorses and trumpeters. The smell of battle, of turned earth and burning bodies filled the room, and Ares stepped out of blood-red smoke.

"Is this your doing?" she asked.

He pulled off his battle gauntlets. "I'm the god of war, not murder." He moved closer, crouching to examine the man. "Perhaps this is Eros's work."

"Eros has not been here. He hasn't left his rooms since he took Psyche to his bed."

"Lucky boy." Ares grinned at her. "A chip off the old block."

"You don't know he's your son. He could just as easily be Hermes'."

"If you could only be faithful, my beauty, then we wouldn't have to have this conversation." He pushed himself up, leather and armor creaking slightly. "Maybe you should stop blaming others for the bad things that happen? Maybe you should look in the mirror?"

"Don't be absurd."

"What is this but love turned and twisted out of shape?"

Aphrodite closed her eyes. "I hate you."

"See. So easy to swing from love to hatred." He pulled his gloves back on. "Come riding with me. I know a place Hephaestus will never find us."

"I am not in the mood for love."

"Then leave love behind and just have sex with me."

She turned slowly, letting her eyes burn, letting her anger boil.

"Ah, my darling. You are surely the most terrifying of any of us." His face was serious for a moment, then he blew her a kiss and disappeared back into his smoke and death.

She wished herself out of the bedroom, to a hillside over the sea — that peaceful, simple realm she had come from. If she had only stayed there, where the rules were clear and she had no special role to play, everything would have been different. But she had wanted more, and Poseidon had been in a mood to indulge her. She hadn't realized that Poseidon had a mean streak; he had to have known what awaited her.

She should have stayed the goddess of foam. Of sea stars and hermit crabs. Of algae and the silver light that danced over the waves at night. But she had been too ambitious.

And now there might be no going back, no matter how much the roar of the waves called to her.

"Great goddess." A woman's voice sounded behind her.

Aphrodite waited for the request that would follow. Only those in search of love could recognize her so easily.

"I am lonely." The woman fell to her knees. "Send me love, I beseech thee."

"You don't know what you ask for. I give it, but love fades. I bless it, and love turns to hate. I rule it, yet love does nothing I say. Love is harder to hold than quicksilver and burns hotter than fire."

The woman stared past Aphrodite, all the way to her someday love. It was clear she could not hear her goddess's words; she was drowning in the soft murmurings of love-that-could-be.

Aphrodite reached down and touched her on the shoulder. "It's yours. Enjoy it while you can."

Before she could see what this woman's love would turn into, she ran like she had not done since she'd first come to land, with legs pumping and head thrown back so the sea breezes blew her hair from her face. She leapt off the cliff, plummeting down, the blue-green waves awaiting her far below.

"You left. You cannot come home." It was Poseidon's voice, cutting through the depths to pierce her with its resolve.

Her descent halted. She felt the winds competing to see who could blow her the fastest. She flew over the land, first west, then south. Then Zephyr took her, heading for Olympus, blowing her through the hallways, down stairs and ramps, until she was deep in the mountain, where Hephaestus lived — where she was supposed to live, too.

For the first time, she realized his workshop's cool darkness was the closest thing to the sea she'd experienced since she'd come to land. It soothed her.

Until she looked at her husband and felt the rush of distaste. It was Zeus's revenge for turning him down when she'd first arrived on Olympus: give the goddess of love a lover she could never want, could never, ever love.

Hephaestus looked up from his forge. His brows pulled down, making him uglier than normal. "You came home?"

"I have no home." She thought of smoke and blood, and the workshop disappeared.

Ares looked up. "Want to take that ride now?"

"Yes." She felt the powerful rush of lust for him, and the love that beat behind it. He was the worst kind of man to want, but even the goddess of love could love unwisely.

In fact, it might be required.

II. The Son

Eros wandered Hephaestus's workroom. He picked up items and studied them, seeing if he could figure out what they were. His uncle had a whimsical nature at times — not everything turned out to be what Eros initially thought.

"Your arrows are almost done."

"Good." He picked up a small sculpture of his mother. "Did you do this?"

"Yes." Hephaestus looked embarrassed. "But I was practicing for something else."

"You can love her. I don't mind."

"Well, she minds, so put that back and tell me about Psyche."

Eros set the sculpture down and sprawled on one of the couches. "She's wonderful."

Hephaestus's face split in a grin, and Eros found it much more appealing than the slick smile of his father. Ares had a way of looking at him like he was a disappointment. Like he could never measure up to his other children. As if Eros would ever want to be like Deimos or Phobos.

"Has your mother accepted Psyche yet?"

"No. Despite being the goddess of love, she can't see true passion when it's right in front of her. I would die for Psyche." There were times he worried that Psyche might die because of him — his mother took controlling to a whole new level.

"Be strong. Aphrodite's a bully like your father."

Eros hated that Hephaestus was right, but he wasn't going to delude himself that his mother wasn't domineering, even cruel, at times. "I don't like that about her."

Hephaestus pounded out the last of the arrows and dunked them into a barrel of water. Steam rose up around him. "She's struggling. I think she'd like to go back to the sea: love isn't quite what she expected."

"I can't believe you're defending her. And she's not like this all the time. She never treats Harmonia this way."

Hephaestus shot him a glance, and Eros swallowed his next words. Harmonia had paid dearly for being Ares' child. Hephaestus had visited no end of trouble on her and her husband. He was finally relenting a little — could bear to hear her name without sparks flying unbidden from his forge.

Eros frowned. Hephaestus never treated him that way, and he'd been born before his sister. "Why do you never get that look when I'm around? You seem to … like having me around."

Hephaestus turned to the forge, but Eros thought he wasn't doing anything all that useful.

"Why don't you hate me, Uncle?"

"You're difficult to hate."

Eros studied Hephaestus's arrows. His uncle had taken one look at the arrows Ares had given Eros and sneered, saying, "Lacking in subtlety as usual."

Then he'd made new ones for Eros. Much finer, invisible to those who'd been shot, and they evaporated once the love spell took.

Eros got up and moved closer. "Ares knows you make these for me."

"So? I'm the better smith — and inventor. He's just a customer, never an originator."

Hephaestus looked proud — proud to have bested Ares? That would make sense after Ares had stolen his wife away and made child after child with her.

Hephaestus looked over at Eros, clearly not expecting Eros to be looking back, and there was a different kind of pride in his face. He looked back down, thrusting a piece of metal into the fire, then grabbing the bellows, working up the flames until it was nearly too hot for Eros.

"Stop it."

"Work to do."

Eros backed away from the fire. "You're hiding."

"Yes, I hide in this cave and make things. You know that."

"No, I mean you are suddenly pretending to be busy, and you never do that when I'm here, so I wonder why." When Hephaestus kept working the bellows, Eros walked over and grabbed his arm, stilling it.

Hephaestus stared at him in what looked like shock — a shock Eros felt, too. There were few who could stop him if he was set on something. Perhaps only his … son?

Eros let go of him. "You're my father, aren't you? It's why I can be faithful to Psyche, not seek other lovers the way Ares would."

"You're talking nonsense." Hephaestus gave him a sharp look. "How could a man so handsome come from my seed?"

"It happens." Eros walked away from the heat of the forge, trying to find a cool spot in the workroom. "I would be proud to call you father."

Hephaestus's steady rhythm with the bellows faltered.

"Very proud."

"You're a good boy. Now, don't you have a new wife at home to make happy?"

"I do." He looked at the statue of his mother. It was an exquisite likeness — even if it caught her in a quiet, almost happy, moment, rather than her usual "when will these mortals learn?" expression.

"If you're so fascinated by that, take it." Hephaestus's voice held a false lightness.

"No, I've got the real thing around all the time." Far more than Psyche wanted her. Eros feared how much more time his mother would spend with them once she found out Psyche was with child.

"I'll leave the statue with you. It's a better version of mother, anyway."

Hephaestus laughed.

As Eros headed for the door, he breathed deeply, absorbing the smell of the smithy. He would bring his child down here, let him or her realize that this place was full of more beauty than all of Olympus.

At the door, he turned; Hephaestus was watching him.

"You're going to be a grandfather. Don't tell mother." He grinned at the smile that lit Hephaestus's face. Such a gentle expression, such joy in a face that normally held pain.

Only the very dim would think this man ugly.

"I won't tell her," Hephaestus said and met Eros's eyes, not hiding the pride in his own. "I'll make the child a rattle."

"I have no doubt that it will be the best rattle ever created."

"Yes," Hephaestus said, "It will."

III. The Grandfather

Hephaestus was dandling Hedone on his lap as she played with the rattle he'd made her. Eros sat on the couch opposite, smiling sleepily at his daughter.

"Close your eyes. Even a god needs some sleep now and then." Hephaestus stood and took the baby around his workroom, and while Eros began to snore, he murmured to her, explaining what each weapon was for, who would use it, and how he had made it special.

Hedone burbled and grasped for the nearest shiny thing, which happened to be a sword, so Hephaestus moved on to less dangerous creations.

He stopped at the sculpture of Aphrodite. "This is your grandmother."

Hedone smiled and reached out. Hephaestus picked the sculpture up and held it close to her. She ran her fingers over Aphrodite's lovely nose, then down her hair. Even in the bronze, you could tell it was golden, each wave intricately carved. He'd touched this statue more than he'd ever touched his wife.

Suddenly he smelled Aphrodite's perfume and turned around.

She was standing at the entrance, and he had to work hard to not stare in longing. She was so beautiful.

But she would never love him — he had to remember that part. The pain of that truth never failed to ground him.

"Eros brought her to you?"

"Well, I didn't kidnap her."

She actually laughed, then she saw her sleeping son and clapped her hand over her mouth as if afraid she would wake him. "She's been fussy, keeping them up."

"So I was told." He turned away and went back to showing Hedone his small treasures. But he could not resist looking over his shoulder and asking his wife, "Would you rather it was Ares holding her?"

"Ares has no time for children." She walked over to them.

Hedone leaned forward and Aphrodite scooped her up, bouncing her for a moment, before letting her lean back to Hephaestus. The child laughed as they repeated the exchange several times.

"She's so beautiful," Hephaestus said.

"She is."

"She takes after you." He tried to keep his face from becoming lovesick after the compliment. Let the statement stand as fact, not flattery.

She smiled, acknowledging his words much more graciously than normal, then she met his eyes. "I do know you're the better man, Hephaestus. I think I'd be happier if I could love you." She looked at the statue, a sorrowful expression on her face.

"Can't force love." He tried to smile and failed. Why couldn't she try? Just once. If she knew he was the better man, why not give him a real chance?

"It's my fault we're stuck with each other." She sighed, brushing back hair so lustrous it rivaled his metalwork. "Zeus was angry with me. He wanted me, and I turned him down. So he gave me to you, to a man he knew I wouldn't love."

Hephaestus laughed. Did she really think this?

"What?"

"He didn't do this to punish you. He did it to punish my mother. To give her son the life she said was what drove her to conceive alone, without his seed. Because she was in love with a man who would never love her back."

Aphrodite turned to him, her expression uncharacteristically soft.

"Don't you see, Aphrodite? I love you with all my heart. I would do anything for you. And you...you do not even like me."

"That's not true."

"This is the longest conversation we've ever had when other people weren't present."

"Eros is present."

"He's dead to the world. We are, for all intents and purposes, alone."

"I could like you, I think. If I didn't feel that I was expected to love you, too."

"I've given up on that. I know when to abandon something, when what I've made won't hold up."

"I wish I knew how to do that." She held her hands out to the baby, and Hedone went to her with a little squeal. "Ares is often cruel."

"He's the god of war, not philanthropy."

She laughed — had she ever laughed this much with him? Then she held the baby out to him, and he took her gently.

"She's my granddaughter, too, isn't she?" He kept his gaze fixed firmly on the child, could not bear to look at his wife if she chose to lie to him.

"Can you imagine the havoc Eros would wreak if Ares were his father?"

He looked up, startled that she would give him so much more than just the answer to his question. "He's not the soul of prudence, even so. He is your son, after all."

She laughed and leaned in to kiss Hedone's cheek, then she settled her hand on Hephaestus's hair. "Maybe this child can make us friends."

"Maybe so."

She walked over to Eros and stood watching him as he slept, then glanced back at Hephaestus.

"I'm sorry I left you out of his life."

"He found his way despite us both."

"He's always understood love, sometimes better than I do, I think." She straightened and closed her eyes, disappearing before him, only the scent of her perfume lingering.

"I love her," he whispered to Hedone.

The baby looked up at him with compassion infinitely beyond her years. She reached up and stroked his cheek, her smile luminous and so full of joy it made Hephaestus laugh.

He held her close and resumed the tour of his workshop, trying to pretend he wasn't concentrating on shelves near where Aphrodite had been standing, where the luscious scent still wafted on the air.

He was love's fool. It was a role that would always hurt, but seemed far less empty now that Eros knew the truth and Hephaestus had this lovely little child in his life.

And maybe his wife. As a friend. Stranger things had happened.

Her Inner Mistress
by Ravenart

Transformation

by Taqerisenu

Her scrubs are sea foam green. Her hair is tied back sensibly. Her voice is firm, and her hands gentle. In practical white sneakers, her feet get restless at the end of the day, tapping out an uneasy heartbeat on colorless linoleum. She thinks of her bed, of a half-read grocery store paperback, of a carton of Lo Mein. Slings her bag up, instead, slipping off her badge, sliding into a changing room.

Her skin feels thin without her scrubs, too tight under the shower's sting. She raises her arms above her head, stretching out the ache of the day. Imagines herself a shape in the steam, face concealed. She thinks of art history, luminescent slides in a dark lecture hall, Paleolithic Venus clasping her limestone breasts, the dimple of her bellybutton in her full moon belly. She thinks of the woman waiting, face concealed, a slumped curve in the plastic hospital chair, hands at her breast clasping a piece of coral, red as ochre-stained stone. She turns off the shower, and puts on a new skin.

There is a ballroom.

Her dress is pink, like the inside of a shell, its edge frothy like sea foam. Her hair is loose, tangling. Her hips sweep and dip, and her hands clasp at sky. In impractical magenta pumps, her feet get restless at the start of the night, tapping out a quickening heartbeat on polished wood. She thinks of her bed, of the press of bodies, of the heady pulse of music thumping behind her breastbone. Throws her head back, then, slipping her hands around shoulders, sliding into the press of the crowd.

Above, the moon is not the same moon it was yesterday. Above, the moon remains.

Soon, she will shed this skin, scrubs and skirts crumpled side by side on the floor, slithering snake-smooth into her sheets, to dream of red ochre and limestone, sea foam and shell pink. As night becomes day, she waxes and wanes, dreaming herself new again.

Rites and Recipes

Aphrodite Ἐρωτοτρόφος (Mother of Love)
by Devon Power

Aphrodite and Modern Pagans

by Amanda Artemisia Forrester

Aphrodite is one of the most immediate Gods. That is because everyone feels Her power. Even those who abstain from sex still have urges. I believe that cultivating a relationship with Her can be extremely rewarding.

I used to have somewhat extreme body issues, and Aphrodite helped me past that. One thing I did was to hang a pretty mirror over my altar, so any time I did ritual I was looking at myself, which I hated to do back then. Seeing my image reflected back at me while I was doing ritual reinforced the belief that as a child of the Gods, I am sacred, and made it more than a mere idea. It took a few months, but it sunk into my psyche, and boosted my self-confidence. I suggest anyone who feels less then beautiful try this, and see how it affects their attitude.

As Pagans, we believe that sex is sacred, not a dirty secret like many monotheist religions teach. But the programming many of us undergo in childhood can be extremely difficult to undo. Working with and worshiping Aphrodite gave me the confidence to flaunt my sexuality and to not feel ashamed for it.

Aphrodite knows that no matter how many lovers you take, you must have time for yourself. Every once in while She would retreat, and the

Three Graces, Her main attendants, would bathe Her with seawater and exotic oils from faraway lands.

Aphrodite teaches us to take time for ourselves, to retreat and pamper ourselves. Take an evening to have a date with yourself. Beginning with a prayer to Aphrodite would be appropriate. Then devote an entire night to your own sensual fulfillment. Be completely self-indulgent. Play soft music and light some candles. Take a long soak in a tub with sweet-smelling bath oils and rose petals scattered on the surface of the water. Drink a glass or two of wine. Enjoy some fragrant lotions, exotic soaps, and soft towels.

After the bath, put on something sexy but comfortable, a loose baby doll nightie, or something sheer. Feel everything, delight in your senses. Concentrate on the feel of the silk sliding across your skin. Run your fingers lightly across your arms, barely touching, a soft breeze almost not there, and you may be surprised at the shiver that runs up your back. Get to know your body.

If it feels appropriate and you want to, you can masturbate. But don't feel that you have to. This is a sensual night, and it need not be sexual unless you want it to be. Just be with yourself, and in your body. Forget about the cares of the day. Refuse to think about work or whatever is causing stress in your life. Focus on your body. You can paint your fingernails or toenails, put on make-up, style your hair, or just lay on the bed listening to music if that's what you like. It's your night, and you can do anything you want.

After a night like that, who could feel ugly? Who could believe that the body is a dirty thing? This is one of the most rejuvenating things I have ever done. Go ahead. Delight in Aphrodite's gifts! Enjoy your body!

Aphrodite Fancy Perfumed Rice Pudding

by Taqerisenu

4 cups 2% milk
4 cups whole milk
1½ cups jasmine rice, rinsed and cooked
2 tsp ground cardamom
2 to 3 Tbsp honey (preferably linden honey. If not, orange blossom or fireweed)
¼ tsp pink himalayan salt
2 tsp rosewater

You'll want to use a very large heavy-bottomed pot for this recipe, such as you might use for making soup. This recipe should produce enough for 8-10 servings.

Pour the milk (both kinds) into the pot, and bring it to a slow, rolling boil. Once it has reached a boil, add the cooked rice, and return it to a boil again. Lower the heat, and let the rice and milk simmer together for about twenty minutes. Make sure to stir the mixture, and that it stays at a low simmer; otherwise, the milk at the very bottom of the pot will begin to scorch and brown.

Add honey to the mixture, to your own taste. The milk and jasmine rice are both naturally sweet in flavor, so you likely won't need more than 3 Tbsp. Add the pink salt, and the ground cardamom. (A word of advice about cardamom: it loses scent and flavor quickly after it is ground, so, if you can, grind your own, or buy it in very small quantities and use it soon after purchase.) Let the mixture simmer for another fifteen to twenty minutes, making sure to stir frequently!

Turn off the heat. Add the rosewater, and stir it into the pudding thoroughly. Let rest for five minutes, and then stir again.

At this point you can either serve the pudding warm, or store it in your fridge to chill, and serve it cold later. I enjoy the pudding both ways, depending on my mood, and how hot or cold the weather is. Additionally, if you would like to, you can top the servings of pudding with cinnamon or ground walnuts.

A Festival of Aphrodite: A Modern Invocation

by Amanda Artemisia Forrester

The first time I performed this ritual, it coincided with the modern celebration of love, Valentine's Day. There are ancient festivals of Aphrodite, but, in my opinion, adapting some of the holidays in our modern calendar to our ritual schedule can be very useful. This is a case of using the over-commercialization of a holiday to our advantage. At this time, everyone, everywhere, is thinking about love. Stores run special deals and sales at this time, so that you can acquire chocolates and teddy bears and other offerings for Aphrodite easily at this time. Seeing the world saturated with these reminders, these symbols, is a powerful thing. To turn this greeting-card holiday into something religious almost makes it seem like the rest of society is celebrating Aphrodite, too. In fact, they are, if not by name. But especially for a lonely Pagan who practices in solitude, this can make it even more meaningful and comforting. However, I specifically wrote this ritual so that it can be performed at anytime. This is a ritual for groups, but could easily be performed alone.

The Ritual

Barley Offering
Sprinkle barley on the altar, saying:

To the givers of life, Life.

Cleansing the Sacred Space

Walk around the ritual space with the khernips bowl, sprinkling the water around the perimeter. Say:

> You are pure! You are pure! By this holy water, this ground is made pure. In the name of Apollo the Purifier this place is cleansed, and is now a holy sanctuary.

Walk in another circle, taking the bowl to each of the worshipers, so they can wash their face and hands. As they are doing so, say:

> By this holy water, you are made pure. In the name the Apollo the Purifier, you are holy and fit to enter the Temple.

Calling of Aphrodite

A worshiper, preferably a woman, calls Aphrodite, saying:

> Hail Aphrodite, primal daughter of the sea!
> Harken to our call, Golden Goddess, and attend our rites
> Lady of love, Lady of All People, we praise You!
> It is Aphrodite who causes love to blossom and passion to burn
> We come together to honor Her for all the loves She has sent our way,

But let us not forget that She is not restricted
     to romantic love
Our Cyprus-born Lady is greater than that
Aphrodite causes the husband to turn to the
     wife
But also the mother to embrace the child
Neighbor to feel friendly towards neighbor
The bonds of brothership to strengthen
And peace to blossom in hearts of all
Greatest Aphrodite, sweet-smelling
      Persuasion

We come before You in awe, daughter of sky
     and sea
We come before You in reverence
We come before You in adoration

We offer to You, Great Goddess, sweet wine
     and rich chocolate
In thanks for all Your gifts.

Calling of Eros
A worshiper, preferably a man or teenage boy, calls
Eros, saying:
     Hail Eros, primal son of the Golden
        Goddess!
     Harken to our call, Great Eros, and attend
        our rites
     Primal Protogenthoi, first-born God
     Though You carry the arrows of love,

You are no mere cherub!
Golden-winged One, the mystery is this:
That You, the primal urge to procreate,
Have existed since the beginning of time,
You Who caused the love of Mother Earth
        and Father Sky,
Yet You are a child born to the Goddess of
        Love
Great Eros, You are a passionate mystery
that is never unraveled!

We come before You in awe, Son of
        Aphrodite!
We come before You in reverence
We come before You in adoration

We offer to You, sweet wine and rich
chocolate, In thanks for all Your gifts.

Sacrament
The Priest/ess passes around the plate of chocolates,
saying:

Before we can truly love another we must
love ourselves. We have to nurture our self-
love before we can offer love to another. As
the the plate of chocolates is passed around,
take a piece as a sacrament.

As you partake, realize that by sharing an
offering with the Goddess, you are taking in
a piece of Aphrodite Herself. Feel Her love

radiate inside you, nurturing your self-love, mindful of the mystery. Remember that you are loved and you are lovable.

Guided by Aphrodite

by Jenny Elliott

I have always looked to Aphrodite for guidance in love and in loving others. A few years ago I was taking a class in which we worked exclusively on her — lessons, meditations, and a Full Moon ceremony. In my Priestess training, I learned how love is not easily found nor is it always beautiful. Reading of Aphrodite's own suffering for love, I did not know what to expect from my devotion, but I discovered the truth and beauty of love — it is not perfect, but is always worth striving for.

The Full Moon ceremony was full of gestures for the great Goddess, including calling in the elements to form the sacred circle, using rose petals to adorn her statue, dancing with her girdle to remember my own sensuality, and offering her honey in thanks. Before we closed the circle, I laid down to soft music and surrendered in meditation to Aphrodite. This was I encountered:

I awoke on a large stone table in a small stone room near dusk. I was bare and felt like a young maiden in my skin. As I lay there, many women in colored robes started to cover me in honey. The smell was intoxicating and its warmth was very relaxing. They were singing sweetly as they soaked my hair in even more honey. They moved away for a few minutes, and returned with baskets of flowers. My senses were bursting with their fragrant tones. The women proceeded to cover me in these amazing flowers, each more beautiful than the last. Only my eyes were free from the flowers.

I stood and was led out of the building, which was by the shore. The sand was a bit pink and the ocean breeze was soft, but constant. The ladies were now dressed in white gowns made of silk. One of them grabbed my hand and led me into a dance around a great fire. I danced with each lady, grabbing her hand as we spun around the circle. As I did, their robes became flowers too, covering the women in nature's beauty.

After the dance, I was led to the ocean, where I was cleansed of the flowers and honey by the ocean's waves. I got back to shore and lay down before the rising moon. I could feel the pull of the moon in the tides around me and inside my heart. Rhythms rocked my soul into a deep slumber. As I started to float away, a band played soft music. I had no fear of drowning as it seemed a force was keeping me safe from the waves and tides. I let go and felt completely loved.

This meditation left me in a state of bliss for the next few days. What amazing love I felt after this initiation! I felt that I was chosen to be one of her daughters and spent the next several nights lighting candles and thanking her for gifting me with such a strong ritual.

My teacher wrote glorious prayers and I used them devotedly during this part of my Priestess training. On another evening, as I was listening to classical music and relaxing, I came face to face with Aphrodite herself. She was a vision in a white robe with a red sash. Her hair was in loose curls and her face shone like a diamond. I had no idea what to do so I just stood in front of her. When she came up to me, I saw tears in her eyes. She spoke of the pain that comes with love, and of the loves we miss from past lives; how no matter how perfect we think love is, there is always a sacrifice to be made and how nothing in this world is assured. I cried at the truth of her words.

Aphrodite then reached for my chest and began to pull out a black substance from my heart. As she reached in, I saw the many ways love had hurt me in the past. How I thought some loved me when their intentions were untrue. How I had not let go of past pain that was obstructing my life in the present. As she pulled out the last of the darkness, I had to let go of those tendrils of sadness and anger. I was no longer that person and to have the past hurt me now was pointless. Aphrodite embraced me as I let out the pain in salty tears, never to dwell on it again.

She then took me to the shore and waded into the water. I walked beside her, so thankful to be free of lingering pain. She then picked up a large shell and placed it inside my chest. It closed over my heart and soon my body healed. I asked her what the shell was for and she said that I was protected from future pain, but must keep thinking ahead and loving who loves me in the present. The sun became unbearably bright and I awoke with amazement at her abundant love and wisdom.

***

Sometimes, we forget the highest love of all: Divine Love. We forget to pour the love back into our own hearts. The deities have love that is beyond the realm of humans. With their love, I have learned to love myself and to be true to the facets of my soul.

Since that time, I have loved deeply and have felt love around me, even when my spirit is low. I have been forever changed by the love of Aphrodite, whom I honor each day. I hope that others learn of her love and cherish this Goddess who is waiting for each of us, at the edge of the shore

Liturgy of Love:
The Liturgia Philotêtos of Epaphroditos
Promulgatio de Ordine Philotêtos
(Proclamation of the Order of Philotês)

by John Opsopaus

Children of the future Age,
Reading this indignant page;
Know that in a former time,
Love! sweet Love! was thought a crime.

— William Blake
"A Little GIRL Lost" (*Songs of Experience*)

Introduction

Empedocles was a Greek shaman (Grk., *iatromantis*) of the fifth century BCE and one of the founders of Greek philosophy (he discovered the four elements). Empedocles explained that there are two great living forces in the universe, which he called Love (Philotês, pronounced *fih-LAW-tays*) and Strife (Neikos, *NAY-koss*). They are associated with Aphrodite and Ares, respectively. According to Hesiod, Love and Strife, offspring of Night (Nux), were ancient deities, predating the Olympians.[16] The original golden age was the Reign of Aphrodite, when all things were united and Love

---

[16] *Theogony*, 224–5, where however Strife is called "Eris."

permeated the length and breadth of the well-rounded cosmic sphere. But Strife, as the River Styx surrounding the Sphere, broke its Unity, and cleaved the One into Many. It divided the four elements, which ever since combine and separate under the opposing actions of Love and Strife to produce the changing world with its manifold objects and qualities. As Heraclitus said, "Through Strife all things come into being."[17] Into the world with Strife came dualism and the tools of discrimination (for good or ill): oaths (sworn on the Styx), bargains, justice, science, and weights and measures.

Empedocles said that Strife also divided the one immortal soul of Love into many individual souls, each encompassing both Love and Strife in some proportion; these immortal souls are reborn time and again into mortal bodies, which are animated by mortal souls compounded from the four elements.

In this day now we have come from the apex of the Reign of Aphrodite to the nadir of the Reign of Ares. We have come from the solidarity of the tribe to the strife of group against group and individual against individual. For Neikos is the attraction of like for like, which separates the four elements and divides people from those unlike

---

[17] Fragment DK 22 B 80.

them; Ares works through jingoism, racism, bigotry, and selfishness.

Aphrodite was called *Pandêmos* — the Goddess of All People — for, like Philotês, she draws together everything, both like and unlike, into One. To return to the Reign of Aphrodite we must invite Philotês into our lives, for Aphrodite does not demand that we be passionate, sexual lovers of everyone else; it is sufficient that we be united by Philotês, whose name means Affection and Friendship as well as Love. She comes when Strife is banished; and whenever we dissolve the divisions between us, we take a step back toward the "well-rounded sphere permeated by Philotês," which was the cosmos of the golden age.

I. Prologue

[1]   Ye Muses, hear!
      For I, Epaphroditus, Hellene, call!
      I beg You! Hear, and grant that I may tell
      my story well! Begin when first appeared
      the goddess, when she came and spoke to me,
      Philotês, Aphrodite's daughter.

[2]   Wretched in my loneliness I called
      the gods on high to help me, hungering
      for human contact after many months
      sequestered for my sacred work,
      the magnum opus, still unfinished.
      Earnestly I asked the gods why love is rare,

for even when we banish Strife, dispel
the fearful force that separates, yet still
the distance is maintained, and Love does not
rush in to fill the vacuum. Thus throughout
the night I burned the sacred incense, poured
libations, pleaded for an answer...

[3]   Becoming drowsy in the deepest night,
      I dozed — just a moment. Startled from
      my sleep I turned, and saw a woman close
      beside me, standing quiet by my side.

      "I am Philotês." This was spoken softly,
      answering the question still behind
      my lips. "Your name means 'Love'," I mused
        out loud.

      "Thou speakest truth," she said, "Dost thou not
        know
      that I'm a goddess? That affection, love,
      and friendship all are mine, the gifts I give?"

[4]   She didn't look to me to be a goddess.
      She was rather short, and had more flesh
      than fit her bones. Her breasts were barely seen
      beneath the rustling drapery of her robe.
      Nor were her clothes divine or rich. She wore
      a simple cotton dress of salmon hue.
      No jewelry adorned her, but a wreath
      of brightly colored flowers ringed her hair,
      of tawny hue, which hung around her neck.

[5]   "Is *this* a love goddess?" I thought again.

Philotês laughed, for she had read my mind.
"My beauty's not so great as some expect."

I blushed at having thus offended her —
a goddess! But she smiled and said, "No need
to fear offense, for vanity is not
my vice, although some other gods have felt
its poisonous sting, and suffered from its bite!

[6] "Attend my words, my friend, for I am not
the same as Aphrodite, she who is
the fountainhead of beauty, charm, and grace.
Although she is my mother, it was not
my lot to have a form that ravisheth.
Nor am I like my brother Eros.
He inherited my mother's beauty and
her passionate heart. He thinketh hardly long
enough to blink before he throweth darts
with wild abandon. Anyway, I think
that you're acquainted long ago with them!"

[7] I laughed and said, "In truth I know them well.
In other times they've sent me many gifts,
such pleasant gifts — and not so pleasant too!"

She smiled and answered, "Thou wilt find my
    gifts
are different; rarely have they been regretted.
Never would I say those other's gifts
are bad, but those who know me, also taste
my gifts, my tender fruit, subdued but sweet."

"What gifts are these?" I asked. Philotês said,
"Attend my words, and thou shalt know them
all."

II. Instruction

[8]   *"Abundant gifts I offer thee,*
but know that they come not for free.
To earn them thou must honor me;
the acts reward the devotee.

[9]   "Attend! Four Sacraments are mine,
the first and second, third and fourth are mine.
For these are holy acts by which thou honor'st
me, but in so doing thou wilt win
my warmth and friendship; thou wilt gain my
gifts
each time thou celebratest these my rites.
Attend and learn my Sacraments of Love."

The First Sacrament

[10] Philotês led me to the mirror, placing
me in my own view; she stood aside
where she could not be seen and spoke these
words:

[11] "The Sacrament of Self is always first.
For know that thou art god and goddess both.

[12] "I call for thee to think upon thy form —
Perhaps my mother, Golden Aphrodite,
gave to thee a share of her own splendor,
the gift of turning heads, of charming hearts,
igniting passions. Gift or curse is this?

Nought cometh free; each blessing is a curse,
each curse a blessing in disguise, at times.

[13] "Whatever portion hath been given thee
of beauty, know that thou art yet a god
and goddess. Look upon thy holy body;
learn to love it. It's a gift of gods
and goddesses to thee. Whatever form
thy gift doth take, yet know it hath been given
thee for thine own pleasure, and for love
of others. Truly, some have been made large
and others small, in whole or in their parts.
And some have coal-dark hair, and others like
the sun, and some have voices sweet to hear,
and others have a forceful tone. The skin
of some is cloaked by copious hair, while some
like infants go, with skin both smooth and
bare.
Whatever characters are thine, are sacred.
Enjoy thine own peculiarities,
and strive to take enjoyment in thyself.

[14] "Again, I say to love thyself!
If thou wouldst love another, or wouldst have
another be in love with thee, then heed
my words, for thou must learn to love thyself.

[15] "Now look upon thy hands, thy arms, thy chest,
thy belly. Feel thy hair, thy fingers, yea,
thy lips, thy breast, thy thighs. Enjoy the feel
of thine own touch.

"Now look upon thy limbs and thy soft parts,
and see them as a font of pleasure and
excitement, for I dwell in everyone.
Thou needest only seek for me, and I'll
enflame desire!

[16] "Now let thy fingers comb thy hair;
enjoy its tangle, thick and soft!

"Now gently, light as feathers, touch thy lips,
and feel my power tingling through thy flesh!

"Now lightly stroke thy breast, so soft beneath
thy palm, and feel thy nipples swell with joy!

"Now lightly rub the mound of thine own
belly,
core of thine existence. Let thy fingers
barely touch the hair between thy legs.

"Now listen! Touch (oh barely touch!) thy sex,
for now is not the time for greater pleasures.
Let thy hand just graze thine inner thigh,
and crack the gates of pleasure. — Enough!

[17] "All this thou knowest well, if only thou
wouldst care to often love thyself, and lose
thyself in every tiny ecstasy,
for then I am with thee!"

The Second Sacrament

[18] "Attend and hear my second sacrament,
the Sacrament of Sight.

[19] "To feast thine eyes upon another's form,
    to savor their sweet scent, and listen in
    delight, devouring their voice, these too
    are sacraments, the pleasures of two people,
    giving and receiving. Thus is Love
    released within the world.

[20] "Whatever form another person hath,
    it hath inherent value. Learn to look
    and see it. Though in vulgar thought their
        beauty
    and attractiveness might never be
    remarked, yet it is there. The more unique
    their form, the more it offereth uncommon
    interest, food for thine appreciation.
    If thou canst not perceive it, then
    the loss is thine.

[21] "The image of another human being,
    in sight or sound, or any other way —
    this is a gift from me, but thou must learn
    to value it. For then the thought or presence
    near of any other person will
    become a source of welcome joy to thee.

[22] "Thou also art a source of joy to others
    in my Order: those who honor me.
    Whatever form the gods have given thee
    is holy; it's a gift from them, through thee,
    to other people wise enough to see.

"If thou wouldst hold the Sacrament of Sight
and worship me, thou shouldst accept the
　　praise
another granteth thee, by eye or ear
or any other way. For I am found
in shared appreciation, joy, affection,
and desire one showeth to another.

[23] "The quick exchange of glances, locking eyes,
the intimate exchange of words, or simply
being near — in little ways like these
I am invoked, and come to stand between
you both, and ye shall feel my warmth, a gift
of me, Philotês, Aphrodite's daughter."

[24] The goddess moved where I could see her, and
she said:

"Now look on me, though I have not the gifts
of Aphrodite, fair in face and form.
But look at me, and see how now I look
at thee — and feel the power grow!
Attend and feel me dwelling in thy flesh.
Now feel my glow throughout thy limbs and
　　loins.
Yes, feel the serpent deep within thee, stirring
from his torpor. Feel his primitive warmth
that spreadeth through thy roots, and feel him
　　stretching
long and hard, and feel him burrowing deep
within thy belly! From the snake take strength
and fortitude. Accept the serpent's gift,

and let the power of life and love increase
within thy loins. The Force between us
   burneth!

[25] "If thou wouldst honor me,
   then learn to give and also take
   the Sacrament of Sight!"

The Third Sacrament

[26] Philotês stepped toward me, drawing close,
   and placed her fingers lightly on my cheek.
   She said, "Now hear the sacrament that's third,
   the Sacrament of Skin.

Touch in My Name

[27] "It's touch that joineth one soul to another;
   learn to touch each other in my name!

[28] "The baby cradled, gently held against
   its mother's breast, to drink warm milk and
     dream.
   Hear: *this* is in my name.

[29] "The child doth gladly wrap his arms around
   another child in close camaraderie.
   And *this* is in my name.

[30] "A woman or a man doth hug their child,
   each winning comfort from the other's love.
   For *this* is in my name.

[31] "Two lovers lightly touch each other's flesh
   and kiss; and if in rapture one doth take

the other in their mouth or belly, *this*,
this too, is in my name.

[32] "For it is I who bringeth each one to
another, trading tenderness and care,
to recognize a bond of common kind,
and join in holy unity."

Be Thou Like a Cat

[33] Philotês put her milk-white arm around
me, bringing me to where my cats sat close
together, grooming one another. "Look,"
she ordered, and we sat beside them.

[34] "Be thou like a cat —
For cats it is enough to lie with other
cats, enjoying their caresses, kissing,
licking more for pleasure than for cleanliness,
for thus all cats are bound together.

[35] "Be thou like a cat —
The cat delighteth rubbing by another.
It will place its head upon a lap
and sleep, and gratefully accept the stroking —
but just so much as pleaseth it!
So, be thou like a cat!"

The Fourth Sacrament

[36] Philotês took me by the hand, and sitting
on the bed, she pulled me down beside
her. Gazing deeply in my eyes she said:

[37] "Of course, I'm happy in the bed where lovers
wrestle; also I'm delighted when
they let their loving partners enter them.
These pleasures too are mine, the sacrament
that's fourth, the Sacrament of Sex.

[38] "Now close thine eyes and turn thy mind
toward
my hands, and feel their warmth against thy
skin.

[39] "Behold the sacred serpent dwelling in
the roots within thy trunk. I will awake
the serpent! Feel the serpent waken! Feel
his muscles tighten, and his thickness swell
and harden. Now uncoiling from his place
of rest, he reacheth out, both long and hungry.
Upward climbing, reaching ever higher,
the serpent stretcheth skyward for his goal.
His rigid length he driveth up the sacred
Tree of Life along the trunk, to find
its bushy foliage, dense and thick with
vigorous
verdant growth. Now high within the leaves
he climbeth, thrusting deep between the limbs,
and stretcheth through their moisture, darkness
which
absorbeth, holdeth Sun's life-giving warmth.

[40] "These gifts I share with Aphrodite and
with Eros, for they are my kin, but there's
a difference. Those who tangle limbs in bed

at *my* request, cement the bonds of people,
even if they never meet again.

[41] "The first one groweth closer to the next,
the second to a third, and so the first
and third grow closer, for each loving act
that's taken in my name, it draweth tight
humanity in mutual affection.

[42] "Now hear this charge I give my devotees,
my family, the members of mine Order:

'Do not forget Philotês name!
Invoke Her through each Sacrament:
of Self, and Sight, and Skin aflame,
and Sex. To each we give assent!'"

III. Initiation

[43] "Thou knowest now my gifts for every mortal
and for thee. When separating Strife
hath gone I'm always willing to arrive,
and draw whomever wishes into warm
embraces of each other — but only if
I'm welcome. Those with whom I'm always
welcome, those I call my loyal Family.
They receive my blessings all the time.

[44] "These are the gifts I offer thee, the boons
of all who join mine Order. Ask thyself
if this could be thy way; think well if thou
wouldst give thy heart to live this way. If it's

thy choice, thou shalt be welcomed to mine
Order."

[45] She spoke no more, but turned her back and
        bowed
her head and waited there. Though overjoyed
by what I'd heard, I kept myself from quick
assent, and pondered the commitments of
her Order, which she called her Family...

[46] At last, when I had clearly seen that there
        was nothing in her Order contrary
to my convictions, I announced my choice.

[47] "Philotês, Goddess, I've decided.
Priceless are the gifts you offer. Gladly
do I promise to attempt to follow
your advice and lead my life thereby."

[48] Philotês turned and smiled; she said, "Well
        chosen
my companion. Listen now and hear
the Sign and Seal by which mine Order's
        joined:

May Love's embrace encircle thee.
I welcome Love; so let it be!

"Remember these, the sacred Sign and Seal!

    'May Love's embrace encircle thee.'

"This is the Sign by which thou mayest seek
my devotees, for they will know the Seal.

    'I welcome Love; so let it be!'

"This is the Seal, and by it thou acceptest
others in the bond of Love; you'll love
each other as is pleasing to you both.

[49] "If thou art firm in thy decision still,
repeat mine Order's Sign and Seal with me:

May Love's embrace encircle thee.
I welcome Love; so let it be!

"Thou hast the Sign and Seal, and knowest
thou
their meaning. Use them well, and use them in
my name."

       She looked me in the eye and asked,
"Art thou prepared to be initiated?"

I answered, "Yes, fair goddess, I'm prepared."

[50] Philotês smiled and loosed the rope around
her robe, which hung unfastened, open down
her right-hand side from arm to floor. The
fabric
fluttered as she walked toward me, and
I thrilled to glimpses of celestial beauty.

Then, smiling kindly, calmly she unloosed
the shoulder clasp, and down around her feet
the saffron robe collapsed in rustling waves.
Dumb-struck I stood before her majesty,
uncertain what to do, or what to say.

[51] "The time hath come to make our troth, for
which

I ask the Fivefold Kiss: first feet, then knees,
then sacred sex, and then my breast and lips."

[52] I trembled as I followed her instructions.
Gently then she stroked my hair and softly
touched my cheek. Becoming more relaxed
I smiled at her. She answered with a smile
and warmly whispered, "Welcome to my
    Family."

"My Goddess, please accept my thanks,"
I answered, bowing in respect.

She smiled again and, pointing to her robe,
politely asked, "If thou wouldst be so kind…"

I draped the simple robe around her sacred
shoulders, and attached the golden clasp.
I stooped and lifted up the rope that was
her belt, and offered it to her, which she
accepted, wrapped around her waist, and
knotted.

IIII. Celebration

[53] Philotês spoke: "The time hath come for thee
to meet some others of mine Order."

With her hand upon my upper arm she turned
me round and I beheld a golden door
with flanking marble columns, glowing white.
As we approached, the golden door swung in.
She brought me through the threshold; there I

saw
a dozen other people, women, men,
of every age and color. They stopped —
They hesitated, looking questioningly.

[54] I stood perplexed until a woman came
to me; she looked into my eyes and said:

"May Love's embrace encircle thee."

With sudden comprehension I replied:

"I welcome Love; so let it be!"

She sweetly laughed and gently touched my
   face.
Uncertain what to do, I stroked her hair;
she stood upon her toes and kissed my cheek.
I looked around and nowhere could I see
   Philotês.
      "Where's the Goddess gone?" I asked.
The woman laughed and said, "She's
   everywhere!"

[55] A slender, grey-haired man approached and
   said,

"May Love's embrace encircle thee."

And I replied with quickly growing trust,

"I welcome Love; so let it be!"

He put his arm around my shoulders, led
me, guiding me toward the others, most
of whom then came and made the sacred Seal.

[56] I saw a shapely woman, standing all
     alone, her golden hair cascading to
     her hips. Approaching her, I said,

"May Love's embrace encircle thee."

"I welcome Love; so let it be!"

she answered with a smile, and so we hugged
in greeting. We admired each other and,
exchanging words, became acquainted well.
And feeling suddenly between my thighs
a motion, I caressed her hair and moved
my lips to hers, but she withdrew from me.
She smiled at my concern, explaining gently,

"The kiss of men is not what I desire;
my lips I'd rather join with my own sex."

I said I understood, apologizing,
but she said there was no need. We spoke
a while some more, and hugged and went our
     ways.

[57] I felt a touch upon my shoulder and
     I turned to see a dark-haired woman, plump
     with Nature's bounty. Doubtfully she spoke,

"May Love's embrace encircle thee."

Philotês stirred my heart and I replied,

"I welcome Love; so let it be!"

We smiled and hugged and I discovered I
enjoyed her soft embrace. Surprising one
another at our friendship, long we talked,

and touched, and sometimes kissed. And once
      when we
embraced, I felt my manhood quickly swell
and stiffen, reaching out to touch her. When
she felt it too, she happily laughed and touched
it softly, sending shudders through my limbs,
and I replied in kind. We traded joy
and pleasure for a while and went our ways.

[58] A man my age approached and made the Sign;
      I made the Seal in answer and embraced
      in greeting. Talking to each other I
      soon noticed that his touches had become
      too intimate for me. I told him so
      politely; he apologized for his
      mistake, and we continued talking for
      a while, and parted with another hug.

[59] I turned and saw a woman watching me;
      our eyes were locked, and neither she nor I
      allowed our gaze to shift before I reached her.

      "May Love's embrace encircle thee."
      "I welcome Love; so let it be!"

[60] Though some might call her features plain, she
      glowed
      with sensuality. She was the first
      to unlock eyes, but only to devour
      by sight my body's every part, and thereby
      I felt free to do the same, and thrill
      my mind with everything I saw of her.
      We spoke in whispers, drawing closer, so

we felt each other's breath, and brought our
    lips
within a hair's breadth. Tentatively hand
touched hand, but soon we pressed our bodies
    tight
together, savoring every strong limb
and every softness. Though we'd never met
before and no doubt never would again,
we wrestled all the more for that, enjoying
every pleasure like it was the last.

V. Epilogue

[61] A spry old woman, laughing, silver haired,
    and holding hands with some much younger
        man,
    addressed the crowd and said:

[62] "Arise ye followers of Philotês!
    Join me in this holy hymn,
    so we may praise our goddess.
    Come, for we're Philotês' Family!"

[63] We sang a song that praised Philotês, fair
    Affection, written by Empedocles,
    a Sage, now gone for many hundred years.
    The hymn we sang is this:

Empedocles' Hymn

[64] "Philotês, thou whose arms surround the world,
    embracing all together, joined as one,

we contemplate thee, who cannot be seen,
and feel thee dwelling in our mortal limbs.
We call thee Friend, for Harmony's thy gift,
and Joy thou'rt named, and Aphrodite too.
When people gather, you arrive unseen;
in lofty clouds you circle like a dove,
and draw us close in bonds of common Love.
Hail, fair Goddess![18]

[65] "In Love all come together,
and desire one another."[19]

[66] We sang, and nestled in another's arms,
I fell asleep, a dreamless bliss.

[67] Much later I awoke; how long I'd been
asleep I cannot tell, but everything
was gone, and I was back within my house.

[68] It's true, I woke! But this was not a dream,
for what Philotês said is surely true,
and since that time our numbers steadily grow,
and we cement our bond with Sign and Seal,
and build our Family as the goddess said.

May Love's embrace encircle thee!

Notes

The *Liturgy of Love* is ©1994 by John Opsopaus
and has been partly serialized, part I in *The Golden*

---

[18] Compare Empedocles' fragment DK 31 B 17 (lines 20–26).

[19] Derived from Empedocles' fragment DK 31 B 21 (line 8).

Apple and the remaining parts in its successor, *Agape* (both now inactive). The introduction is from my *Exercise for Unity*, available at the Biblioteca Arcana; visit omphalos.org/BA.

Bibliography

Inwood, Brad (1992). *The Poem of Empedocles: A Text and Translation with an Introduction.* Toronto: Univ. of Toronto Press.

Wright, M. R. (1981). *Empedocles: The Extant Fragments.* New Haven: Yale Univ. Press.

Offerings for Aphrodite

by Amanda Artemisia Forrester

[Excerpted from the forthcoming *Journey to Olympos: A Modern Spiritual Odyssey*]

You may want to set up an altar to Aphrodite, separate from your main altar. Mine is located in the bedroom, next to my bed. Drape it with a beautiful cloth, perhaps something rich like silk or velvet, in deep colors like red or purple. Arrange flowers, real or artificial, into pleasing arrangements. Seashells or stars are beautiful and appropriate accents. African cowie shells resemble female genitals, adding another layer of meaning. Some scented candles, beautiful antique bottles of perfumes, or bowls of potpourri help set the mood. You could even place a few sex manuals on the altar. Whatever you do, make the altar as beautiful and pleasing as you can. Aphrodite will appreciate the effort, and you will have fun doing it.

When thinking of what offerings Aphrodite would enjoy, the first thing to spring to mind would be the red rose. The red rose was one of her most sacred plants[20]. Today it still retains its reputation for being connected to love, as it is the traditional gift lovers give each other. But many other plants were also considered sacred to her. Among them are

---

[20] Greek Lyric II The Anacreontea, Frag 35, Greek Lyric II *The Anacreontea*, Frag 44, Apuleius. *The Golden Ass* 4.2

the apple[21], such as the golden one that started the Trojan War, myrrh[22], the tree from which Adonis was born, the anemone flower[23], which sprang from the blood of Adonis, narcissus[24], myrtle[25], and cinnamon[26].

Aphrodite has many sacred animals as well. Dove[27], swallow[28], or sparrow[29] feathers would also a very appropriate offering, as they are Her sacred birds. Fish[30], and especially the shellfish[31], are sacred to Aphrodite as well. She is a Sea-Goddess,

[21] Pausanias. *Guide to Greece* 2.10.4, Philostratus the Elder. *Imagines* 1.6, Suidas "Rhamnousia Nemesis"

[22] Aelian. *On Animals* 10. 34, Apuleius. *The Golden Ass* 6. 6 ff

[23] Nonnus. *Dionysiaca* 32.10,

[24] Aesop. Fables 205 (from Phaedrus 3.17), Pausanias. *Guide to Greece* 5.13.7, Virgil. *Georgics* 1.27

[25] Ovid. *Metamorphoses* 10.705, Nonnus. *Dionysiaca* 32.10,

[26] Apuleius. *The Golden Ass* 2. 8 ff

[27] Aelian. *On Animals* 10.33, Ovid. *Metamorphoses* 14.597 Apuleius. *The Golden Ass* 6.6, Nonnus. *Dionysiaca*, 33.4

[28] Aelian. *On Animals* 10.34

[29] Nonnus. *Dionysiaca* 33.4

[30] Hyginus. *Astronomica* 2.30, Ovid. *Fasti* 2.458, Ovid. *Metamorphoses* 5.319

[31] Athenaeus. *Deipnosophistae* 3.88a, Nonnus. *Dionysiaca* 32.10

after all. The rabbit[32] with its unquenchable libido is definitely Hers.

For a slightly more expensive offering, the pearl was considered the gemstone of Aphrodite[33] and referred to as "the stone of love". There are always, of course, libations of honey, wine, and fine oils as well.

Offerings need not be rooted in Greek practice, either. Aphrodite is a Goddess Who thoroughly enjoys every sensation. She exalts in every pleasure. Think. What does the modern world offer that Aphrodite would enjoy? Perhaps gourmet chocolate, scented massage oils, fuck-me high heels, sultry make-up, silky lingerie, or even sex toys. These are just a few ideas.

If you are artistic, draw or paint an erotic scene. Write love poetry. Remember what it was that made you fall for your partner in the first place. One exercise I did to thank Aphrodite for sending me my (then)partner was to make a list of everything I loved about him and our relationship. The list included trivial and even silly things, as well as deeper things. I listed his beautiful, deep blue eyes and gorgeous waist-length hair alongside his patience, his screwy sense of humor, his determination to work through our problems, his fanatical devotion to Halloween haunted houses,

---

[32] Philostratus the Elder. *Imagines* 1.6

[33] Nonnus. *Dionysiaca* 32.10

and his ingeniousness. It was a wonderful exercise that made me fall in love with him all over again. Which was the whole point. The list ended up having 167 separate things, with extra space to write more down as I thought of them. It was a part of my altar to the Love Gods for as long as we were together.

Become a matchmaker, helping other people to find love as well. Dress in a sexy and becoming manner, but be sure that you are comfortable. Don't dress too loudly; Aphrodite hates crassness. Flirt! But always remember to take care of yourself. Don't be afraid to claim "me time." Make your home as beautiful and welcoming as possible. Endeavor to constantly have at least one vase with fresh flowers in your home. Experience new sensations, smells and tastes. Support sex-workers and safer sex practices.

Of course, making love is one of the most powerful offerings, and the most fun! Dedicate your pleasure, and your partner's, to the Goddess as a gift and a thank-you. Read the Kama Sutra and other ancient sexual manuals. Learn new techniques. Explore Tantra and sex magic, if you are so inclined.

Remember, simply being in love, either with yourself, a lover, or the whole world, is the best offering you can give Her. And, in the end, it is the gift She gives you back.

Three Prayers to Aphrodite

by Rev. Donna M. Swindells

Morning Prayer to Aphrodite: I welcome you, Aphrodite, as the morning star, shining your blessings upon your daughter. O Golden One, you who are a daughter of sky & sea, reign over all creation with your loving presence. I ask you to protect my heart from those who are unworthy of its love. Teach me to be free, as you are, to love those who pull at our heartstrings. To be unrestrained & restricted by no one. Let me be Master of the secrets of my heart. Give me the tools of seduction & persuasion, to use with care. Enchantress, this day I give you my love, knowing it is the gift you most treasure & desire. Blessed be Aphrodite, daughter of Titans and Queen of all hearts!

Evening Prayer to Aphrodite: The Golden Sun gives way to the evening star, shining above all. I call to you, beloved Star of the sea. You are known as "Stella Maris" a beacon for those who sail the sea. You rise & shine as Venus, as the Moon itself reflects your glory. Aphrodite, let my heart find a safe harbor in which to secure my heart. May my secret desires be satisfied as night blankets the sky with stars. Let me wrap myself in beauty, and may bliss find me ready to receive its kiss.

Night Prayer: Aphrodite, violet crowned Goddess of love, I give you my last kiss. I send it to the heavens, where you reign as its Queen. Come, enter my humble Temple. Smell the sweet myrrh incense that rises up for you. See my candle burning on my altar. Its flame reflects my love for you. I call to you, as a Priestess & lover. I wear rose oil, anointing myself as your property. I play soft music to soothe you. I adorn myself to receive you. Come, the hour is late. I await you here, or in my dreams.

Tannhauser and Venus
by John Collier

Publication Credits

"Fox" originally published online 17/06/16 by **Three Drops from a Cauldron Journal** *(Issue One)*

"Sappho and the Woman of Starlight" previously published in **Eternal Haunted Summer** *(Winter Solstice 2016). Rhysling 2017 nominee.*

Appendix A:
Public Domain Texts

Homeric Hymn 5 to Aphrodite (translated by Hugh Evelyn-White) (Greek epic C7th to 4th B.C.)
Moisa (Muse), tell me the deeds of golden Aphrodite Kypria (Cyprian), who stirs up sweet passion in the gods and subdues the tribes of mortal men and birds that fly in air and all the many creatures that the dry land rears, and all the sea: all these love the deeds of rich-crowned Kythereia.

[The story of the love of Aphrodite and Ankhises follows.]

Hail, goddess, queen of well-builded Kypros (Cyprus)! With you have I begun; now I will turn me to another hymn.

***

Homeric Hymn 6 to Aphrodite
"I will sing of stately Aphrodite, gold-crowned and beautiful, whose dominion is the walled cities of all sea-set Kypros (Cyprus). There the moist breath of Zephyros the western wind wafted her over the waves of the loud-moaning sea in soft foam, ad there the gold-filleted Horai (Horae, Seasons) welcomed her joyously.

[The story of the birth of Aphrodite follows.]
Hail, sweetly-winning, coy-eyed goddess! Grant that I may gain the victory in this contest, and order you my song. And now I will remember you and another song also.

***

Homeric Hymn 10 to Aphrodite
Of Kythereia (Cytherea) [Aphrodite], born in Kypros (Cyprus), I will sing. She gives kindly gifts to men: smiles are ever on her lovely face, and lovely is the brightness that plays over it. Hail, goddess, queen of well-built Salamis and sea-girt Kypros; grant me a cheerful song. And now I will remember you and another song also.

***

Orphic Hymn 55 to Aphrodite (translated by Thomas Taylor) (Greek hymns C3rd B.C. to 2nd A.D.)
To Aphrodite. Ourania (Urania) (Heavenly), illustrious, laughter-loving (*philommeideia*) queen, sea-born (*pontogenes*), night-loving (*philopannyx*), of awful mien; crafty, from whom Ananke (Necessity) first came, producing, nightly, all-connecting dame. 'Tis thine the world with harmony to join, for all things spring from thee, O power divine. The triple Moirai (Fates) are ruled by thy decree, and all productions yield alike to thee:

whatever the heavens, encircling all, contain, earth fruit-producing, and the stormy main, thy sway confesses, and obeys thy nod, awful attendant of Bakkhos [Dionysos] God. Goddess of marriage, charming to the sight, mother of the Erotes (Loves), whom banquetings delight; source of Peitho (Persuasion), secret, favouring queen, illustrious born, apparent and unseen; spousal Lukaina, and to men inclined, prolific, most-desired, life-giving, kind. Great sceptre-bearer of the Gods, 'tis thine mortals in necessary bands to join; and every tribe of savage monsters dire in magic chains to bind through mad desire. Come, Kyprogenes (Cyprus-Born), and to my prayer incline, whether exalted in the heavens you shine, or pleased in odorous Syria to preside, or over the Aigyptian (Egyptian) plains they care to guide, fashioned of gold; and near its sacred flood, fertile and famed, to fix they blest abode; or if rejoicing in the azure shores, near where the sea with foaming billows roars, the circling choirs of mortals thy delight, or beauteous Nymphai (Nymphs) with eyes cerulean bright, pleased by the sandy banks renowned of old, to drive thy rapid two-yoked car of gold; or if in Kypros (Cyprus) thy famed mother fair, where Nymphai unmarried praise thee every year, the loveliest Nymphai, who in the chorus join, Adonis pure to sing, and thee divine. Come, all-attractive, to my prayer inclined, for thee I call, with holy, reverent mind.

***

Apuleius, The Golden Ass 10. 30 ff (trans. Walsh)
(Roman novel 2nd century A.D.)

[From a description of an ancient Greek play portraying the Judgement of Paris:] After them a third girl entered, her beauty visibly unsurpassed. Her charming, ambrosia-like complexion intimated that she represented the earlier Venus [Aphrodite] when that goddess was still a maiden. She vaunted her unblemished beauty by appearing naked and unclothed except for a thin silken garment veiling her entrancing lower parts. An inquisitive gust of air would at one moment with quite lubricous affection blow this garment aside, so that when wafted away it revealed her virgin bloom; at another moment it would wantonly breathe directly upon it, clinging tightly and vividly outlining the pleasurable prospect of her lower limbs. The goddess's appearance offered contrasting colours to the eye, for her body was dazzling white, intimating her descent from heaven and her robe was dark blue, denoting her emergence from the sea . . .

Each maiden representing a goddess was accompanied by her own escort ... Venus [Aphrodite] was surrounded by a throng of the happiest children; you would have sworn that those little boys whose skins were smooth and milk-white were genuine Cupides [Erotes] who had just flown in from sky or sea. They looked just he part with their tiny wings, miniature arrows, and the rest of their get-up, as with gleaming torches they lit the way for their mistress as though she were en route to a wedding-banquet. Next floated in charming children, unmarried girls, representing on one side the Gratiae [Charites, Graces] at their most graceful, and on the other the Horae [Horai] in all their beauty. They were appeasing the goddess by strewing wreaths and single blossoms before her, and they formed a most elegant chorus-line as they sought to please the Mistress of pleasures with the foliage of spring. The flutes with their many stops were now rendering in sweet harmony melodies in the Lydian mode. As they affectingly softened the hearts of onlookers, Venus [Aphrodite] still more affectingly began to gently stir herself; with gradual, lingering steps, restrained swaying of the hips, and slow inclination of the head she began to advance, her refined movements matching the soft wounds of the flutes. Occasionally her eyes alone would dance, as at one moment she gently lowered her lids, and at another imperiously signalled with threatening glances.

***

Stasinus of Cyprus or Hegesias of Aegina, Cypria Fragment 6 (from Athenaeus 15. 682) (trans. by Hugh Evelyn-White) (Greek epic C7th or 6th B.C.)
She [Aphrodite] clothed herself with garments which the Kharites (Charites, Graces) and Horai

(Hours) had made for her and dyed in flowers of spring — such flowers as the Horai (Horae, Seasons) wear — in crocus and hyacinth and flourishing violet and the rose's lovely bloom, so sweet and delicious, and heavenly buds, the flowers of the narcissus and lily. In such perfumed garments is Aphrodite clothed at all seasons.

***

Virgil. Eclogues, Georgics, Aeneid (trans. by Fairclough, H R. Loeb Classical Library Volumes 63 & 64. Cambridge, MA. Harvard University Press. 1916.)
[1 : 223] Now all was ended, when from the sky's summit Jupiter looked forth upon the sail-winged sea and outspread lands, the shores and peoples far and wide, and, looking, paused on heaven's height and cast his eyes on Libya's realm. And lo! as on such cares he pondered in heart, Venus, saddened and her bright eyes brimming with tears, spoke to him: "You that with eternal sway rule the world of men and gods, and frighten with your bolt, what great crime could my Aeneas – could my Trojans – have wrought against you, to whom, after many disasters borne, the whole world is barred for Italy's sake? Surely it was your promise that from them some time, as the years rolled on, the Romans were to arise; from them, even from Teucer's restored line, should come rulers to hold the sea and all lands beneath their sway. What thought, father, ahs turned

you? That promise, indeed, was my comfort for Troy's fall and sad overthrow, when I weighed fate against the fates opposed. Now, though tried by so many disasters, the same fortune dogs them. What end of their toils, great king, do you grant? Antenor could escape the Achaean host, thread safely the Illyrian gulfs and inmost realms of the Liburnians, and pass the springs of Timavus, and whence through nine mouths, with a mountain's mighty roar, it comes a bursting flood and buries the fields under its sounding sea. Yet here he set Padua's town, a home for his Teucrians, gave a name to the race, and hung up the arms of Troy; now, settled in tranquil peace, he is at rest. But we, your offspring, to whom you grant the heights of heaven, have lost our ships – O shame unutterable! – and, to appease one angry foe, are betrayed and kept far from Italian shores. And thus is piety honoured? Is this the way you restore us to empire?

***

The Judgment of Venus by Matthew Prior
When Kneller's works, of various grace,
Were to fair Venus shown,
The Goddess spied in every face
Some features of her own.

Just so, (and pointing with her hand)
So shone, says she, my eyes,
When from two goddesses I gain'd

An apple for a prize.

When in the glass and river too
My face I lately view'd,
Such was I, if the glass be true,
If true the crystal flood.

In colours of this glorious kind
Apelles painted me;
My hair, thus flowing with the wind
Sprung from my native sea.

Like this disorder'd, wild, forlorn,
Big with ten thousand fears,
Thee, my Adonis, did I mourn
E'en beautiful in tears.

But viewing Myra placed apart,
I fear, says she, I fear,
Appelles, that Sir Godfrey's art
Has far surpass'd thine here:

Or I, a goddess of the skies,
By Mary am undone,
And must resign to her the prize,
The apple, which I won.

But soon as she had Myra seen,
Majestically fair,
The sparkling eye, the look serene,
The gay and easy air.

With fiery emulation fill'd
The wondering goddess cried,
Apelles must to Kneller yield,
Or Venus must to Hyde.

Appendix B:
Epithets of Aphrodite

compiled by Chelsea Luellon Bolton

Aligena (Sea Born)
Ambologera (She Who Postpones Old Age)
Anaduomene (Rising from the Sea)
Androphonos (Killer of Men)
Anosia (Unholy)
Apatouros (Deceptive One)
Apostrophia (She Who Turns Herself Away)
Apostrophia (Averter of Unlawful Desires)
Areia (Warlike; of Ares)
Basilis (Queen)
Dôritis (Bountiful)
Eleemon (Merciful)
Enoplios (Bearing Weapons)
Epipontia (On the Sea)
Epistrophia (She Who Turns to Love)
Epitragidia (She Upon the Buck)
Epitumbidia (She Upon the Graves)
Euplois (Fair Sailing)
Euploia (Fair Voyage)
Genetullis (Genetrix)
Heteira (Courtesan)
Hera (of Hera; of Marriage)
Hôplismenê (Armed)
Kallipugos (of the Beautiful Buttocks)
Kallisti (the Fairest)
Kataskopia (Spying; Peeping)

Khruse (Golden)
Kupris (Cyprian)
Kuprogenes (Cyprus-born)
Kuthereia (Kytherean)
Limenia (of the Harbor)
Makhanitis (Deviser; Contriver)
Mechanitis (Skilled in Inventing)
Melainis (Black)
Migôntis (Marital Union)
Morpho (Shapely Form)
Nikêphoros (Bringer of Victory)
Nymphia (Bridal)
Ourania (Heavenly)
Pandemos (of All People)
Pasiphaessa (the Far-Shining)
Pelagia (of the Sea)
Philomeides (Laughter-Loving)
Porne (Fleshy; Prostitute)
Potnia (of the Sea)
Praxis (Action; Sexual)
Psithyristês (Whispering)
Skotia (Dark)
Suriê theos-Syrian Goddess
Summakhia (Ally in War)
Symmakhia (Ally in Love)
Tumborukhos (Gravedigger)
Xenia (of the Foreigner)

Homeric Epithets
Kythereia (of Cytherea Island)
Kyprogenês (Born in Cyprus)

Kyprogeneia (Born in Cyprus)
Kypris (of Cyprus)
Paphia (of Paphos in Cyprus)
Paphiê (of Paphos in Cyprus)
Diôniaia (Daughter of Dione)

Homeric Epithets 2
Aphrogeneia (Foam-Born)
Aphrogenês (Foam-Born)
Dia (Divine; Shining)
Dios thugatêr (Daughter of Zeus)
Eustephanos (Richly-Crowned; Well-Girdled)
Khryseê (Golden)
Philommeidês (Laughter-Loving)
Philomeidês (Laughter-Loving)
Philommedes (Genital Loving)
Pothôn Mêtêr (Mother of Desire)

English Epithets for Aphrodite
Mistress of Animals

Cult and Festival Terms
Aphrodision (Temple of Aphrodite)
Aphrodisia (Festival of Aphrodite)
Adônia (Festival of Adonis and Aphrodite)
Hystêria (Festival of the Swine)
Anagôgia (Festival of Embarkation)

Sources

Theoi.com: Aphrodite Titles

Aphrodite at Neos Alexandria

Burkett, Walter. *Greek Religion*. John Raffan, trans. Harvard University Press, 1985.

Cyrino, Monica S. *Aphrodite. (Gods and Heroes of the Ancient World Series)*. Routledge, 2010.

Appendix C:
Our Contributors

Alexeigynaix is a poet, artist, crafter, and Hellenion clergy education student. You may find their work at alexeigynaix.wordpress.com and etsy.com/shop/sunbowarts; they also run Delmarva Nikephoros Proto-Demos of Hellenion, which may be found at delmarvanikephoros.wordpress.com.

Chelsea Luellon Bolton has a BA and MA in Religious Studies from the University of South Florida. She is the author of *Lady of Praise, Lady of Power: Ancient Hymns of the Goddess Aset*, *Queen of the Road: Poetry of the Goddess Aset*, and *Magician, Mother and Queen: A Research Paper on the Goddess Aset*. She is the editor and a contributor of the forthcoming anthology *She Who Speaks Through Silence: A Devotional Anthology for Nebet Het (Nephthys)*. Her poetry has been previously published in various anthologies. She lives with tons of books and her anti-social feline companion. You can read more of her work at her blog address: http://fiercelybrightone.com

Merit Brokaw is a librarian, housewife, mother, wife, writer, crafter, woman and devotee to the gods of her heart. Like an octopus, she is making her way through the sea of life, following wherever curiosity takes her.

Rebecca Buchanan is the editor of the Pagan literary ezine, *Eternal Haunted Summer*, as well as the editor-in-chief of *Bibliotheca Alexandrina*. She has been published in a wide variety of venues and has released two short story collections, *A Witch Among Wolves, And Other Pagan Tales*; and *The Serpent in the Throat, And Other Pagan Tales* (*Asphodel Press*).

A devotional polytheist for over twenty-five years, **Edward Butler** received his doctorate from the New School for Social Research in 2004 for his dissertation "The Metaphysics of Polytheism in Proclus." Since then, he has published numerous articles in academic journals and edited volumes, primarily on Platonism and on polytheistic philosophy of religion, as well as contributing essays to several devotional volumes. He is also an associate editor of *Walking the Worlds: A Biannual Journal of Polytheism and Spiritwork*. Much more information on his work can be found at his site, Henadology: Philosophy and Theology (henadology.wordpress.com).

Ashley Dioses is a writer of dark fantasy, horror, and weird poetry from southern California. Her debut collection of dark traditional poetry, *Diary of a Sorceress*, is forthcoming from *Hippocampus Press* in 2018. Her poetry has appeared in *Weird Fiction Review*, *Spectral Realms*, *Weirdbook Magazine*, and elsewhere. Her poem "Carathis," published in *Spectral Realms 1*, appeared in Ellen Datlow's full recommended *Best Horror of the Year* Volume Seven list. She has also appeared in the *Horror Writers Association Poetry Showcase 2016* for her poem "Ghoul Mistress." She is an Active member in the HWA and a member of the SFPA. She blogs at fiendlover.blogspot.com.

Jenny Elliott is a Hierophant of Hekate in The Fellowship of Isis and lives in Richmond, Virginia with her husband, Jason. She has contributed to *Circle Magazine* and two previous devotionals for *Bibliotheca Alexandrina*: *Lunessence: A Devotional to Selene* and *Daughter of the Sun: A Devotional Anthology in Honor of Sekhmet*. In her spare time, she likes to read, paint, write poetry, honor her ancestors, work on rituals with various deities for Dark and Full Moons as well as the Sabbaths, offers services to the local pagan community, and loves spending time with her family. You can contact her at facebook.com/HekatesLady

Pegi Eyers is the author of *Ancient Spirit Rising: Reclaiming Your Roots & Restoring Earth Community*, an examination of the interface between Turtle Island First Nations and the Settler Society, social justice work, rejecting Empire, and the vital recovery of our own ancestral earth-connected knowledge and essential eco-selves. She is a member of the Celtic mtDNA-based Helena Clan (world clans descended from "Mitochondrial

Eve" as traced by *The Seven Daughters of Eve*), with more recent roots connecting her to the mythic arts and pagan traditions of both England and Scotland. She lives in the countryside on the outskirts of Peterborough, Canada on a hilltop with views reaching for miles in all directions. www.stonecirclepress.com.

Amanda Artemisia Forrester is currently working on building the Missouri homestead of her dreams. She is the author of 'Ink In My Veins: A Collection of Contemporary Pagan Poetry', and 'Songs of Praise: Hymns to the Gods of Greece'. She is working on the forthcoming 'Journey to Olympos: A Modern Spiritual Odyssey'. A self-labeled history geek, she has taught classes on Greek Mythology, contacting your spirit guides, and has written and taught the coursework for "Olympos in Egypt", an introduction to the unique hybrid culture and spiritually that grew up in Alexandria, Egypt in the Hellenistic Age. In a few years when the homestead is up and running, she may make it her goal to begin teaching again and holding rituals on her 5 acre property, Artemis Acres, and reestablish the Temple of Athena the Savior (formerly of South Bend, Indiana) in Missouri. Her blog can be found at templeofathena.wordpress.com, and she runs a Cafepress store, OtherWorld Creations, at cafepress.com/other_world.

Mary Geschwindt enjoys participating in a variety of creative endeavors. As an architecture student, she devotes her free time to writing poetry. In addition to her poetry, Mary serves on the editorial team for *CRIT Magazine*, a national journal dedicated to student architectural work and ideas. Her poetry has also been featured in the online publication of *Rookie Mag*.

Laurie Goodhart is both painter and farmer. With feet in the soil and head in the stars, her hands leave all kinds of traces. Plenty of the less ephemeral are visible at lauriegoodhart.net.

Anne Graue lives in New York and is the author of *Fig Tree in Winter* (*Dancing Girl Press*, 2017). Her work has appeared in numerous journals including the *Westchester Review, The 5-2 Crime Poetry Weekly, The Ginosko Literary Review,* the *Plath Poetry Project,* and the *Margaret Atwood Society Journal*. She is a writing instructor as well as a reviewer for *NewPages.com*.

Lori Anne Gravley lives with her husband, two dogs, and thirteen stringed instruments. Sometimes her sons come to visit. She grew up in Niceville, Florida; earned her MFA in El Paso, Texas; and now she lives in Yellow Springs, Ohio, at the edges of fields which sometimes (in the dark after snow) look like dunes and waving sea oats and sometimes look like buffalo grass and desert sand. She has been nominated for a Pushcart and Best New Poets and has poems, published and forthcoming, in a number of journals and anthologies, including *Bitterzoet*, *Appalachian Heritage*, and *Jabberwock Review*.

Robert F. Gross is a writer, theatrical director, and performer. His works have appeared recently in *RPD Society*, *Tigershark*, *Sein und Werden*, and *Anti-Heroin Chic*. He's currently residing in Rochester, New York.

Deborah Guzzi writes full time; when she's not reading. She is a candidate for the 2015 Science Fiction Poetry Association's Rhysling Award. Her book, ***The Hurricane,*** published by *Prolific Press* is now available. She travels the world seeking writing inspiration. She has walked the Great Wall of China, seen Nepal (during the civil war), Japan, Egypt (two weeks before 'The Arab Spring'), Peru, and France during December's terrorist attacks. Her poetry appears in: *Existere - Journal of Arts and Literature* in Canada, *Tincture* in Australia, *Cha: Asian Literary Review*, China, *Vine Leaves Literary Journal* in Greece, and *Eye to the Telescope*, *Bete Noir*, *Liquid Imagination*, *Illumen*, *Literary Hatchet*, and *Silver Blade,* among others, in the USA.

Leni Hester is a writer, ritualist and Witch living in Denver, Colorado where she serves the Orisas and the Ancestors. Her work has appeared in *Manifesting Prosperity*, *Women's Voices in Magick*, and *Pop Culture Grimoire*, all from *Immanion Press*, and in *Queen of the Great Below*, *Bearing Torches*, *First and Last*, and *The Dark Ones* from *Bibliotheca Alexandrina*. Leni also blogs on "Season and Spirit" at Pagan Square, and has been a regular contributor to *Sagewoman* and *witches&pagans* for over fifteen years. Trained in the Western Mystery Tradition, Wicca (Gardnerian and Alexandrian lines), Lukumi, yoga, and the sacred arts of dance and theatre, Leni brings a lifetime of occult exploration, experimentation and devotion to all her work.

An artist, author, ritualist, presenter, and spiritual seeker, **Shauna Aura Knight** travels nationally offering intensive education in the transformative arts of ritual, community leadership, and personal growth. She is the author of *The Leader Within*, *Ritual Facilitation*, and *Dreamwork for the Initiate's Path*, and co-editor of the P*agan Leadership Anthology*. Her writing is included in several blogs and Pagan magazines, and her work appears in numerous anthologies including *Pagan Consent Culture*, *Bringing Race to the Table*, *Stepping in to Ourselves*, and more. She's also the author of urban fantasy and paranormal romance novels including *The Truth Upon Her Lips*, *A Fading Amaranth*, *A Winter Knight's Vigil*, *Werewolves in the Kitchen*, *Werewolves with Chocolate*, and more. Shauna's mythic artwork and designs are used for magazine covers, book covers, and illustrations, as well as decorating many walls, shrines, and other spaces. Shauna is passionate about creating rituals, experiences, spaces, stories, and artwork to awaken mythic imagination. See her work at http://www.shaunaauraknight.com

Terence Kuch's fiction, poetry, and non-fiction has been published in the U.S., U.K., Canada, Ireland, Australia, Europe, and Asia, including *Commonweal, Diagram, Dissent, Gravel, Grub Street, Mademoiselle, The Moth, New Scientist, North American Review, Poetry Motel, Sheepshead Review, Thema, Timber Creek Review, Washington Post Book World, Washington Post Magazine*, and *Yellow Mama*. His novel, *The Seventh Effect*, was praised by *Kirkus Reviews*. A satirical poem of his won first prize in a New York magazine competition, was praised and reprinted in the *New York Times*, and included in a *Random House*-published collection. He studied at the Writers Center, Bethesda, Maryland, and participated in the Mid-American Review Summer Fiction Workshop.

David W. Landrum teaches English at Grand Valley Sate University in Allendale, Michigan. His speculative fiction has appeared in *Garden of the Goddesses, New Myths, Non-Binary Review, Pedestal Magazine, Woman of Fire/Woman of Snow*, and many other journals and anthologies. His latest novella, *The Sorceress of the Northern Seas*, is available online.

Jennifer Lawrence has followed the gods of Greece, Ireland, and the Northlands for decades now; she is a member of Hellenion, The Troth, Ár nDraíocht Féin, and Ord Brigideach. After earning a B.A. in Literature and a B.S. in Criminal Justice, she went on to work as an editor for Jupiter Gardens Press, a small publishing company in the Midwest. Her interests include history, gardening, herbalism, mythology and fairy tales, hiking, camping, and the martial arts. Her work has appeared in numerous publications, including *Aphelion*, *Jabberwocky*, *Cabinet Des Fees*, *Goblin Fruit*, *Idunna*, *Oak Leaves,* and many devotional anthologies. She lives with five cats, an overgrown garden full of nature spirits, and a houseful of gargoyles somewhere outside of Chicago.

Gerri Leen lives in Northern Virginia and originally hails from Seattle. She has work appearing in: *Nature,* Flame Tree Press's *Murder Mayhem* and *Dystopia Utopia* anthologies, *Daily Science Fiction*, *Escape Pod*, *Grimdark,* and others. She recently caught the editing bug and has finalized her third anthology for an independent press. See more at http://www.gerrileen.com.

Marc Littman is a former journalist who has penned many life-affirming short stories plus two novels, Eddie and Me On the Scrap Heap about a heroic boy who has autism and The Spirit Sherpa, a mystery novel with a reincarnation twist.

Kyler Luffy is a writer, photographer, and student living in the bustle and rain of the Pacific Northwest. He's been contributing to various publications for two years, recently turning his pen to reflect on the more personal topics of religion, love and loss.

Iona Miller is a nonfiction writer widely published in the academic and popular press, clinical hypnotherapist, and multimedia artist. She is interested in archetypes, myth, ancestors, and dreams as well as the experiences and effects of doctrines of religion, science, philosophy, psychology, and the arts. She has a long history of professional participation and teaching in Personal Mythology. Her work has appeared in other NA devotionals. http://ionamiller.weebly.com

Allie Nelson is an aspiring poet, novelist, and conservationist who is passionate about nature and the modern mythic. Former Poetry Editor at the College of William and Mary's *Gallery* magazine, her works have been published in various anthologies and journals including *Apex Magazine*, *Eternal Haunted Summer*, Folk Horror Revival's *Corpse Roads* anthology, *POWER Magazine*, and *Renewable Energy World*. She is currently hard at work on too many novels, a chapbook, and grad school.

Dr. John "Apollonius" Opsopaus has practiced magic and divination since the 1960s, during which time he has studied theurgy and other ancient forms of magic, tarot and other divination systems, Pythagoreanism and other esoteric disciplines, and spiritual alchemy. His fiction (hymns, poetry, and prose) and nonfiction (rituals, translations, divination systems, essays) have been published in various magical and Neopagan magazines (over 30 publications). Based on his research he designed the Pythagorean Tarot and wrote the comprehensive *Guide to the Pythagorean Tarot* (Llewellyn, 2001). He presents workshops on Hellenic magic and Neopaganism, Pythagorean theurgy and spiritual practices, divination, and related topics.

Opsopaus has been involved in the magical and Neopagan communities on-line for twenty years, and his Biblioteca Arcana website (omphalos.org/BA) has won numerous awards and is featured in several Internet guides. In 1995 he founded the Omphalos, a networking organization for Neopagans in the Greek and Roman Traditions and one of the first internet resources especially for them. Opsopaus is past coordinator of the Scholars Guild for the Church of All Worlds, past Arkhon of the Hellenic Kin of ADF (A Druid Fellowship), and past Dean of the Department of Ceremonial Magick of the Grey School of Wizardry. Opsopaus is a member of the Grey Council and is listed under "Who's Who in the Wiccan Community" in Gerina Dunwich's *Wicca Source Book* (Citadel, 1996). He explains ancient divination in *The Oracles of Apollo* (*Llewellyn*, 2017).

Richard King Perkins II is a state-sponsored advocate for residents in long-term care facilities. He lives in Crystal Lake, IL, USA with his wife, Vickie and daughter, Sage. He is a three-time Pushcart, Best of the Net and Best of the Web nominee whose work has appeared in more than a thousand publications including The Louisiana Review, Plainsongs, Texas Review, Hawai'i Review, Roanoke Review, Sugar House Review and The William and Mary Review. His poem "Grease Poet" was a recent prize winner of the Woodrow Hall award for enduring excellence in poetry. His poem "Nemesis" recently won the Songs Of Eretz Editor's Choice award.

Devon Power opted not to provide a biography.

Ravenart, the Prince of Painters, once had the Muses appear to him. Sent by Lady Athena, Lady Aphrodite and Lord Apollo, they gave him Homer's staff. The Muses said to him, make us the art in bold poetic color and dramatic lines that capture the heroic energy of life. The full-throated force that exists in this Gods-infused world, full of crowded life in all its sensual zeal. Make us art that will awaken this generation to the glory of the living Gods and the glory of this vital world full of beauty and life . So commissioned, he went forth to create art with his inspired hands in the Western tradition inherited from the ancient Greeks. Art that, with Father Zeus' blessing, he pursues to bring new glory to the Gods and the ancestors of old. He now lives in New York City with his familiar raven who has kept him company since his boyhood. His website is www.RavenartStudio.com

Michael Routery is a polytheist poet and writer living in Hawai'i. He's the author of *From the Prow of Myth* (Vindos Press), a collection of devotional poetry. His Pagan writings can be found in various Bibliotheca Alexandrina devotional anthologies, as well as in Scarlet Imprint's *Mandragora*, and *Datura*, and in *A Beautiful Resistance*. He also writes for the Celtic reconstructionist magazine *Air n-Aithesc*. A Druid and practitioner of the Irish filidecht poetry tradition, he also worships various Greek deities. Michael has an MFA in Creative Writing and blogs at finnchuillsmast at wordpress.

K.S. Roy (also known as Khryseis Astra) is an artist, astrologer, and writer living in Western Pennsylvania. She is particularly devoted to Hekate, Hermes, Persephone, Apollon, and the Muses. She has been the Graphic Designer for *He Epistole*, a Hellenic Polytheist newsletter issued by Neokoroi, the editor for *Guardian of the Road: A Devotional Anthology in Honor of Hermes,* and is currently at work on a devotional art series for the Theoi.

John W. Sexton lives in the Republic of Ireland and is a Muse pagan. He is the author of five poetry collections, the most recent being *Petit Mal* (Revival Press, 2009) and *The Offspring of the Moon* (Salmon Poetry, 2013). His sixth collection, *Futures Pass*, is forthcoming from Salmon in late 2017. His two YA novels, *The Johnny Coffin Diaries* and *Johnny Coffin School-Dazed*, have been published in Ireland by the O'Brien Press and have been translated into Italian and Serbian. Under the ironic pseudonym of Sex W. Johnston he has recorded an album with legendary Stranglers frontman, Hugh Cornwell, entitled *Sons of Shiva*, which has been released on Track Records. He is a past nominee for The Hennessy Literary Award and his poem "The Green Owl" won the Listowel Poetry Prize 2007. Also in 2007 he was awarded a Patrick and Katherine Kavanagh Fellowship in Poetry.

Beate Sigriddaughter, www.sigriddaughter.com, is poet laureate of Silver City, New Mexico (Land of Enchantment). Her work has received several Pushcart Prize nominations and poetry awards. In 2018 *FutureCycle Press* will publish her poetry collection *Xanthippe and Her Friends,* and *Červená*

Barva Press will publish her chapbook *Dancing in Santa Fe and Other Poems* in 2019.

Rodopi Sisamis lives in Brooklyn, NY, with hellion triplets, a shadow dog, a twice reincarnated cat, and a kitten named after Emily Bronte. She has been published in *She Walks in Shadows*, *Daughter of the Sun*, *The Queen of the Sky that Rules Over All the Gods*, and other anthologies. She is also the author of *Elysium: Modern Myths of Immortality* which is her first short story compilation.

David Subacchi lives in Wales where he was born of Italian roots. He studied at the University of Liverpool and he has four published collections of his English Language poetry: *First Cut* (2012), *Hiding in Shadows* (2014), *Not Really a Stranger* (2016), and *A Terrible Beauty* (2016). His work has also appeared in numerous literary magazines and anthologies. You can find out more about David and his work here: http://www.writeoutloud.net/profiles/davidsubacchi.

Reverend Donna M. Swindells is a licensed reverend in the Fellowship of Isis. A Priestess of Dionysus and a Hierophant of Hathor, she teaches two FOI chartered schools of spirituality: the Iseum of Hathor, Lady of the West and Lyceum of Dionysus, Ariadne, and Aphrodite, Star of the Sea. You can follow her spiritual blog, Walking the Mystic's path at ibgreenie3dot.com.wordpress.com.

Taqerisenu is a museum professional living in Seattle. She is a Shemsu of the Kemetic Orthodox faith. She has loved ancient Egyptian mythology and culture since she was a toddler, and her mother had to pull her away from the television, where she'd been enraptured by a recording of Aida that was playing on the local PBS channel (Egypt > bedtime, clearly). She likes to think deeply about time travel, digital technology as a tool for informal learning, mythology, ancient cookery, and Sherlock Holmes. Her poetry has also been published in the *Bibliotheca Alexandrina* anthologies *Garland of the Goddess: Tales and Poems of the Feminine Divine, The Dark Ones: Tales and Poems of the Shadow Gods,* and *Dauntless:A Devotional for Ares and Mars.*

Jinny Webber, Professor Emerita, Santa Barbara City College, continues to teach literature courses in extended learning programs on Shakespeare, British literature, and mythological topics. She writes plays for DramaDogs of Santa Barbara, and historical fiction, primarily set in Elizabethan England and occasionally Bronze Age Greece. "Becoming a Priestess of Aphrodite" is based on the early chapters of her unpublished novel, *Serpent Wisdom: The Story of Teiresias*. Visit www.jinnywebber.com.

Shannon Connor Winward is the author of the Elgin-award winning chapbook, *Undoing Winter*. Her writing has appeared in *Fantasy & Science*

Fiction, Analog, The Pedestal Magazine, Pseudopod, Eternal Haunted Summer, Mirror Dance, Star*Line, and elsewhere. In between writing, parenting, and other madness, Shannon is also an officer for the Science Fiction Poetry Association, a poetry editor for *Devilfish Review* and founding editor of *Riddled with Arrows Literary Journal.*

Gareth Writer-Davies: Commended in the Prole Laureate Competition, the Welsh Poetry Competition and Commended in the Sherborne Open Poetry Competition (2015). Shortlisted for the Bridport Prize and the Erbacce Prize (2014). His pamphlet *Bodies* was published in 2015 by *Indigo Dreams* and his next pamphlet, *Cry Baby*, will come out this year. He is the Prole Laureate for 2017.

Appendix D:
About Bibliotheca Alexandrina

Ptolemy Soter, the first Makedonian ruler of Egypt, established the library at Alexandria to collect all of the world's learning in a single place. His scholars compiled definitive editions of the Classics, translated important foreign texts into Greek, and made monumental strides in science, mathematics, philosophy and literature. By some accounts over a million scrolls were housed in the famed library, and though it has long since perished due to the ravages of war, fire, and human ignorance, the image of this great institution has remained as a powerful inspiration down through the centuries.

To help promote the revival of traditional polytheistic religions we have launched a series of books dedicated to the ancient gods of Greece and Egypt. The library is a collaborative effort drawing on the combined resources of the different elements within the modern Hellenic and Kemetic communities, in the hope that we can come together to praise our gods and share our diverse understandings, experiences and approaches to the divine.

A list of our current and forthcoming titles can be found on the following page. For more information on the Bibliotheca, our submission requirements for upcoming devotionals, or to learn about our organization, please visit us at neosalexandria.org.

Sincerely,

The Editorial Board
of the Library of Neos Alexandria

Current Titles

Written in Wine: A Devotional Anthology for Dionysos

Dancing God: Poetry of Myths and Magicks

Goat Foot God

Longing for Wisdom: The Message of the Maxims

The Phillupic Hymns

Unbound: A Devotional Anthology for Artemis

Waters of Life: A Devotional Anthology for Isis and Serapis

Bearing Torches: A Devotional Anthology for Hekate

Queen of the Great Below: An Anthology in Honor of Ereshkigal

From Cave to Sky: A Devotional Anthology in Honor of Zeus

Out of Arcadia: A Devotional Anthology for Pan

Anointed: A Devotional Anthology for the Deities of the Near and Middle East

The Scribing Ibis: An Anthology of Pagan Fiction in Honor of Thoth

Queen of the Sacred Way: A Devotional Anthology in Honor of Persephone

Unto Herself: A Devotional Anthology for Independent Goddesses

The Shining Cities: An Anthology of Pagan Science Fiction

Guardian of the Road: A Devotional Anthology in Honor of Hermes

Harnessing Fire: A Devotional Anthology in Honor of Hephaestus

Beyond the Pillars: An Anthology of Pagan Fantasy

Queen of Olympos: A Devotional Anthology for Hera and Iuno

A Mantle of Stars: A Devotional Anthology in Honor of the Queen of Heaven

Crossing the River: An Anthology in Honor of Sacred Journeys

Ferryman of Souls: A Devotional for Charon

By Blood, Bone, and Blade: A Tribute to the Morrigan

Potnia: An Anthology in Honor of Demeter

The Queen of the Sky Who Rules Over All the Gods: A Devotional Anthology in Honor of Bast

From the Roaring Deep: A Devotional for Poseidon and the Spirits of the Sea

Daughter of the Sun: A Devotional Anthology in Honor of Sekhmet

Seasons of Grace: A Devotional in Honor of the Muses, the Charites, and the Horae

Lunessence: A Devotional for Selene

Les Cabinets des Polythéistes: An Anthology of Pagan Fairy Tales, Folktales, and Nursery Rhymes

With Lyre and Bow: A Devotional in Honor of Apollo

Garland of the Goddess: Tales and Poems of the Feminine Divine

The Dark Ones: Tales and Poems of the Shadow Gods

First and Last: A Devotional for Hestia

Dauntless: A Devotional in Honor of Ares and Mars

Blood and Roses: A Devotional for Aphrodite and Venus

Forthcoming Titles

At the Gates of Dawn and Dusk: A Devotional for Eos and Aurora

The Far-Shining One: A Devotional for Helios and the Spirits of the Sun

A Silver Sun and Inky Clouds: A Devotional for Djehuty and Set

Lord of the Carnelian Temple: A Devotional in Honor of Sobek

Lord of the Horizon: A Devotional in Honor of Horus

Made in the USA
Coppell, TX
04 July 2020

30151596R00171